FOR
SABBATH'S
SAKE

Embracing
Your Need for
Rest, Worship, and
Community

J. DANA TRENT

UPPER
ROOM BO
NASHVILLE

Upper Room Books® website: books.upperroom.org

Cover design: Bruce Gore
Interior design and typesetting: PerfecType | Nashville, TN

Library of Congress Cataloging-in-Publication Data
Names: Trent, J. Dana, author.
Title: For Sabbath's sake : embracing your need for rest, worship, and community / J. Dana Trent.
Description: Nashville : Upper Room Books, 2017. |
Identifiers: LCCN 2016056673 (print) | LCCN 2017036724 (ebook) | ISBN 9780835817202 (Mobi) | ISBN 9780835817219 (Epub) | ISBN 9780835817196 (print)
Subjects: LCSH: Rest—Religious aspects—Christianity. | Worship. | Sabbath. | Sunday.
Classification: LCC BV4597.55 (ebook) | LCC BV4597.55 .T74 2017 (print) | DDC 263/.3—dc23
LC record available at https://lccn.loc.gov/2016056673

Printed in the United States of America

For Judy and Gail, two little girls who refused
to go to the movies on the sabbath
and
for you who long for sabbath, may you find rest,
devotion, and community in these pages.

Grant me grace this day
to rest and remember
that there is nothing I have to do,
nothing I have to buy or sell,
nothing I have to produce or consume
in order to become who I already am:
your beloved creation.
    May your overworked creation
    and those who cannot rest today
    come to know the liberation of your sabbath.
           —Sam Hamilton-Poore, *Earth Gospel*

CONTENTS

ACKNOWLEDGMENTS

A book isn't written in isolation. It's a village affair, a push-pull of introversion and extroversion, of both closing and opening the door. When the door was open, countless saints contributed to this project. My family and friends kept me sane and encouraged; they generously shared their love and wisdom.

Many thanks to my mother, Judy Trent, and Aunt "Gangsta" Gail Shelton, who held firm in their sabbath beliefs and instilled them in me. I'm indebted to Fred Eaker, who helps me keep sacred time. Much gratitude is owed to Kate Rademacher, who inspired this book and assisted in its content. Countless cheers to Rabbi Larry Bach, whose wisdom urges me to lean into the ancient "spiritual technology" that sabbath offers.

I'm grateful for my fellow writers who provided guest posts in late 2014 for my blog series "Stealing Back Sabbath." Kate Rademacher, Kristen E. Vincent, and Rev. Jennifer Hege all planted seeds for these chapters.

Many clergypersons anonymously contributed their authentic reflections on the challenges and opportunities of observing sabbath in parish life. Additionally, Susan Mitzner, Vanna Fox, Aunt Gloria "Glo" Eaker, and Judy Harrow graciously shared their specific spiritual practices, along with many on social media who offered suggestions and tips.

Many thanks to the faith communities that formed me. They walk the talk, continuing to shape me—and many others—so that I am accountable in both faith and life. I especially give thanks to God for Dana Community Bible Church, First Baptist Church Reidsville, Binkley Baptist Church, and Sri Caitanya Sanga.

I continue to be blessed by a collaboration with Upper Room Books. A book is only as good as its editor, and this one owes its life to Joanna Bradley.

1

Q-TIPS AND BOTOX

The Sabbath is a day for the sake of life.
—ABRAHAM JOSHUA HESCHEL, *THE SABBATH*

Last year, I lost a Q-tip in my ear.

I'd been making the bed, rehearsing lesson plans, brushing my teeth, and mindlessly bobbing a cotton swab in and out of my head. I was already ten minutes late for work when I saw the asymmetrical stick in the trash can. I bent over and felt a tickle. An awkward ear selfie revealed that the cotton tail had disappeared into my skull.

Oh well, I thought. *It's not a big deal. It's not like it's going anywhere.*

I texted my husband, Fred, as I sat in traffic, and he called me.

"Is the *entire* Q-tip stuck in your ear?"

"Nope. Just the end thingy."

"The what?"

"The tail thing, the cotton thing, the swab thing, the whatev—"

"You need to go to urgent care *immediately*," he said. I could hear him typing in the background.

"Like right now? I've got to teach."

"Go!" he urged. "You can't just leave a Q-tip in your ear. You could lose your hearing."

"What?" I said.

"Hearing loss! You could lose your hearing!"

"Huh?"

"Call me when you're done," he said and hung up.

I recruited the college librarian as an emergency substitute for my freshman composition class. An hour later, a physician's assistant removed the fluffy culprit.

"You need to slow down," she sighed, shaking her head. "Read this." She handed me a compulsory pamphlet on preventing foreign objects from getting lodged in facial orifices—a guide for parents whose toddlers shove rocks up their noses.

My students clapped when I returned to campus. I'd survived *another* ridiculous disaster. Just two weeks prior, I'd forgotten how to conjugate irregular verbs in my mother tongue. "I have *readed* your essays," I said to twenty-five perplexed eighteen-year-olds. They were used to my flustered self—always stressed out and often distracted—but that semester had been particularly bad for me. I was working four part-time jobs in three counties, frequently interrupting lectures to retrieve a silver tube of peppermint essential oil to roll over my brow. The oil usually dripped into my eyes, rendering me temporarily visually impaired. My students giggled while I taught with my eyes closed. I used the oil so often that they dubbed it my "crack stick."

Stressed Out

I am a *migraineur*, a fancy term for people who sometimes feel as though ice picks are being driven into their brains. Nearly thirty-eight million Americans suffer from migraines, creating a multibillion-dollar industry to treat them. My migraines can be caused by anything: light, food, smells, weather changes, hormone fluctuations, too much sleep, too little sleep, too much screen time, and intense conversations. Most recently, the status of my illness progressed to *chronic migraine*, which means I spend half my life feeling like I have an ax in my head.

"Lighten up," people suggested, chalking up my condition to perfectionism and spreading myself too thin. For them, the solution seemed easy, but I'd tried everything: relaxing, praying, meditating, over-the-counter medications, prescription medications, acupuncture, acupressure, yoga, herbal steam baths, ice therapy, heat therapy, and a meager diet of leaves and air. Cinnamon paste often covered my forehead, and I swallowed tablespoons of Sriracha with a lemon water and pink Himalayan salt chaser. The peppermint "crack stick" was acceptable in public; a suspicious brown substance smeared on my face not so much.

In the midst of my almost daily migraines, I continued to work, to care for my mother suffering from dementia, and to provide volunteer pastoral care because I felt I had to. My chronic migraine diagnosis urged me to take on more. I didn't want to be viewed as weak or compromised by my health. I put on a strong face, but all I wanted to do was hide in a cold, lavender-infused basement.

At the height of my condition, my neurologist suggested I participate in a clinical study, comparing the effects of two FDA-approved chronic migraine medications: Topomax, an anti-seizure drug, and Botox. Famous for its nearly eight hundred medical uses, Botox (botulinum toxin) is most commonly utilized for erasing wrinkles. When used for migraines, both Topomax and Botox ease the frequency of chronic migraine, ideally putting the patient's condition into "remission." The study would offer me access to free medication and careful monitoring. I was sick enough to try anything, including donating my head and time to science and exposing myself to possible botulism poisoning.

The study randomized me to Topomax first, which works brilliantly for many but terribly for others. For six weeks, I powered through, determined to make the anti-convulsant medication my Holy Grail. I lost ten pounds (not a bad side effect) but lived with constant tingling in my hands and toes, forgot my own language, suffered from a perpetual cold, and became depressed. Later, when I'd discontinued my use of Topomax, I heard a neurologist interviewed by National Public Radio call it "Dopomax," citing its massive list of side effects, including cognitive impairment.

Deciding that my body's negative reaction to the medication far outweighed any reduction in migraines, the clinical study coordinator switched me to Botox. I would receive thirty-two injections quarterly in my neck, scalp, temples, and forehead. According to the research, I'd either have fewer migraines and the wrinkle-free forehead of a twenty-year-old or continued migraines and facial paralysis. Hoping for my miracle cure, I muddled on. After several rounds of Botox, my migraine severity and frequency decreased. Episodes that typically rendered me useless were further apart. I was not cured, but my life felt less interrupted. I began to see an existence beyond being sick.

My chronic condition meant I needed continued medical treatment, but I also knew I needed to lean into another way of life. Living through Topomax's side effects made me realize I was trying to fight physical decline and depression with avoidance and busyness instead of self-care. But those weren't holistic solutions. My migraines had always been less severe during seasons of my life when I was *both* on the correct medication *and* calm and connected—more attuned to my soul, God, and community. In addition to the clinical study, I needed a spiritual elixir. Instead of forcing myself into a Wonder Woman suit, I needed to make time for rest. Medicine works best in tandem with balancing the human essentials: enough sleep, nutritious foods, and stable homelife. I needed to get my condition under control while seeking meaningful relationships with God and others. The symptoms—migraines, depression, busyness—were indications of something larger. The chronic condition that dictated my days became an invitation to find peace and purpose beyond deadlines and success.

I remembered times when I wasn't so stressed—when weekly replenishment hadn't seemed so out of reach. Two decades ago, when the world was much different, time felt slow and limitless. I had no migraines; I spent many guilt-free Sundays with no worldly goal in sight, filling my hours with daydreaming, reading, resting, praising, praying, fellowshiping, gathering, and moving toward the Divine. Time had been my most abundant resource. Back then, I seemed to understand the medicinal value of free time.

Sabbath Girls

High Point, North Carolina, has hosted the famous biannual furniture market since 1906. Internationally renowned, it is the largest home furnishings industry trade show in the world, boasting 11.5 million square feet, two thousand exhibitors, and seventy-five thousand attendees per year.

The market is not open to the public. But during one market season in the 1950s, my Great-Uncle Seldon secured Sunday admission tickets for his wife, my Great-Aunt Frances, whom he called "Miss Fronsus," and her sister, my Grandmother Evelyn. The two rural women were delighted, and they crafted a plan. They would take my mother and her older sister, Gail, to the thirty-five-cent Sunday matinee and then go drool over exclusive home furnishings.

"Girls, mother and Aunt Frances are going to the market this afternoon. We're going to drop you off at the picture show," Grandmother Evelyn proclaimed. My mother and her sister were puzzled—not the reaction the adults expected. "Girls, we thought you'd be *delighted* to see a movie today," Grandmother Evelyn urged.

"But we *don't* go to the movies on Sundays," the girls said, confused.

"It's alright. You can do it just this once."

Judy and Gail, the youngest of my Grandmother Evelyn's five children, stood their ground, respectful but unwavering. "But we *don't* go to the movies on the sabbath," they repeated, reciting the commandment they'd heard on so many Sundays of their lives. They knew the Genesis Creation story backward and forward—a rhythm of six and one, working and ceasing.

"Girls, it's okay just for today. Uncle Seldon got us these special tickets. Go on now, get in the car." But the girls wouldn't budge, and Grandmother Evelyn and Great-Aunt Frances never made it to the furniture market.

The adults, after all, had taught their children that the sabbath was the Lord's Day, not theirs. Its hours were holy, which meant no movies, no card games, and no dancing to records on the side porch. The sabbath was a day different from all the rest—a day for ceasing from any labor and worldly activity one might do the remaining six days of the week. Only church, acts of service, family visits, and resting were permitted.

Grandmother Evelyn and Great-Aunt Frances watched their once-in-a-lifetime opportunity disappear before their eyes thanks to two little girls who'd learned their Sunday school lessons a little too well.

Easy Like Sunday Morning

The women on both sides of my family had learned the "church first" mantra from their mothers, all staunch Christian women. In generations prior to mine, though people still worked themselves to the bone, American culture was more conducive to ceasing from labor and consumption on Sundays. Anyone who grew up in a small town remembers when merchants rolled up the sidewalks on Saturday night. In my mother's and grandmothers' eras, gas tanks and liquor cabinets were filled before Sunday. All errands were completed ahead of the Lord's Day, even for people who weren't particularly religious. In that time, Sunday school—not youth soccer leagues—heralded the new week. After church, tables were dressed in fine linens and china. Families enjoyed the rhythm of a slow, shared meal. People talked with one another, face-to-face, before a feast with enough cholesterol to flip the food pyramid. Eye contact was abundant, liquor was sneaked, town gossip was shared, and children exhausted their patience waiting for something interesting to happen. The TV was silent; no video games or iPads vied for kids' attention. Smartphones and the Internet didn't exist. Sweet gospel hymns at Sunday Vespers rounded out the day, and the week was off to a stellar start.

Grandmother Evelyn labored over her Sunday supper fixings Saturday night so that the only work she did on the sabbath was place a hen in the oven before church. Occasionally, she invited friends to her Sunday meal, but mostly the day was spent with family. Afterward, she shooed her husband and five children away for the only respite she had all week: reading the newspaper on the couch, the one time her family ever saw her put her feet up.

In keeping with ceasing from her labors, Grandmother Evelyn nick-named her Sunday evening meal "Every Man for Himself." This meant her dependents had to battle one another for the lunch leftovers. It was the only meal she didn't prepare all week. By evening, she loaded her five children into the station wagon for church services and visits to the county home, where the despondent waited for cheery company to arrive. Grandmother Evelyn trained her offspring to deliver love and smiles to these elderly shut-ins because Jesus had commanded them to do so "for the least of these."

Some Sundays, Grandmother Evelyn drove my mother and her sib-lings down country back roads to visit their grandmother, my Great-Grandmother Jettie, who also made weekly Sunday lunches. Once the table was set, Grandma Jettie covered her dining room table with a bed sheet to keep the flies away, and the children were invited to sneak pieces of deep-fried goodness when they arrived. The meal and family stayed all day; there was no urgency for refrigeration or goodbyes.

During my mother's afternoons there, Grandma Jettie would station herself on the front porch, where she rocked and crocheted. She accepted visitors, and her grandchildren sat with her one by one, amused by her ability to drink an entire carton of glass Pepsi bottles in several hours. Later, when diabetes took hold of Jettie's body, she moved in with Grand-mother Evelyn and the children. At age eight, my mother's nursing career began when she learned how to administer Jettie's insulin shots.

Life in the 1940s and 1950s had its ups and downs; the world was both a mess and bursting with seeds of progress. There was bounty and poverty, peace and war, understanding and prejudice. No matter what happened outside the home, one truth remained for the Trent family: They lived by strict sabbath rules. No one made any Sunday plans unless they involved Jesus or family. With some modern adaptations in place, I spent my early life following the same guidelines.

Glory Days

In 1980, my newlywed parents migrated from Ohio to Los Angeles to conceive their "California Girl." Because of fertility issues and a doctor's advice, my parents decided they needed warmer weather and less stress to get pregnant. On their way to California, they saw a rainbow, which they took as a sign. My mother delivered one year later, shortly after her forty-first birthday. My parents mailed a pink Hollywood movie stub to relatives to announce my birth.

My mother and father believed I was destined to live a glamorous life of fame. But the recession and poverty forced them out of California and back to the familiar and less expensive towns of their youth. I was only three months old when we arrived in Dana, Indiana, to live in a trailer adjacent to my grandparents' house.

My first six years were spent in Dana and Clinton, whose combined populations could fit in a large high school football stadium. My parents divorced when I was six, and Mom and I moved to Chapel Hill, North Carolina, which I considered an upgrade since the town boasted more than one grocery store inside the city limits. But my earliest sabbath formation began in the place for which I was named, a township with a slow pace.

Let My Day Begin with Saraluia

My first sabbaths spent in Dana were with my Midwestern paternal family, who lived and worked among the rural Indiana cornfields. My paternal grandmother, Dorothy, was a WWII veteran and nurse. She and my Grandfather Richard had shuffled their three rowdy boys to the Dana Community Bible Church, which they had helped charter in the 1950s.

After my parents divorced, I returned to Indiana each summer to live with my Grandmother and Grandfather Lewman (whom I called G and GL). They made me and my cousins, Britainy and Erin, keep the same rhythm my father and his brothers had known as children.

G and GL woke early on Sundays and dressed to the nines. They turned on TV preachers and prodded their three granddaughters from bed. Grandfather laid out quarters for us girls to place in the offering plate, and Grandmother let us spray ourselves with her Chloé perfume and apply strawberry Chapstick at her vanity table.

Dana Community Bible Church's Sunday school began at *"9:30 sharp!"*—an actual song my cousins and I were taught that I'm convinced was composed as propaganda to get children and families to church on time. As we arrived, we'd belt: *"9:30 sharp! 9:30 sharp! I will be at Sunday school 9:30 sharp!"*

My cousins (who are like sisters to me) and I thought church was fun. Answering Bible trivia correctly meant retrieving a plastic prize from an enormous cardboard box decorated with biblical wrapping paper. We'd rehearse song lyrics written on poster board to sing before the forty-person congregation at the start of "big church." We knew these church songs as well as we knew "Rudolph, the Red-Nosed Reindeer," and we took poetic license in keeping them entertaining. The church's organist at the time, a woman named Saralu, played as we sang loudly and off-key, *"Let my day begin with alleluia . . ."* Only we substituted *alleluia* with *Saraluia*, breaking into fits of giggles.

Even before we knew its spiritual purpose, church was a jovial affair, a brilliant tactic to make certain that kids and parents *wanted* to be in the pews. The Lewman Family alone took up two large, orange-fabric ones. After the children sang our (adapted) songs, my cousins and I stood with my aunt, my uncle, my father, and G and GL as the five-person choir led us through hymns. We shouted them out, trying to keep up with Grandmother Dorothy's charming but froggy voice, which was low and boisterous. During scripture readings, Britainy, Erin, and I passed notes on the bulletin, and we couldn't contain ourselves when Grandmother snored through the sermon. After services, we returned to G and GL's for lunch, or they drove us across the Wabash River to Montezuma, where we ate broasted potatoes and strawberry fluff at Janet's Restaurant.

In the afternoon, G and GL napped in the living room with newspapers on their chests. The girls and I tiptoed out the garage door for long bike rides to the outskirts of Dana, which was only 0.3 square miles. On warm days, we swam in Uncle Jon and Aunt Phyllis's pool. We entertained ourselves for hours, and a sabbath afternoon could stretch out infinitely. A delicious midafternoon nap felt like an entire night's worth of sleep. We invented games with bikes and sang along to the *Dirty Dancing* soundtrack, indulging in the luxury now known as *boredom*.

Junior Sabbatarian

From Dana Community Bible Church onward, I was raised as a sabbatarian. After my parents divorced, my mother and I moved to Chapel Hill, North Carolina, a small, intellectual town whose churches were more highbrow than my corn-town "Saraluia" songs would have allowed. Binkley Baptist Church became our new sabbath home. Mom worked weekend night shifts as a nurse, but she made certain my babysitters got me to church as much as possible.

My mother and I lived in Chapel Hill until the early 90s, when Mom went broke and we needed a soft (and free) place to land. Her hometown of Reidsville, North Carolina, was the perfect fit. I was twelve when we began attending First Baptist Church, Grandmother Evelyn's parish. First Baptist Church is where I learned once again to lean into Sunday afternoon ennui, knowing that youth group activities were only hours away. Sundays brought respite from the Monday through Friday flurry of homework, peer pressure, and school drama. I spent my teen years in a wood-paneled bedroom on Main Street, kissing magazine cutouts of Keanu Reeves and dancing to the 1993 Salt-N-Pepa album, *Very Necessary*. Sundays included no extracurricular activities outside of worshiping Jesus. Any social plans I made were sacred ones, and my Swatch watch ensured I never missed the half-mile commute to church. Any inattention I felt during service could be attributed to daydreaming about crushes rather than worrying about any to-do lists. Even when I was sick, skipping church left me uneasy, like I'd missed a weekly dose of medicine.

Like the Dana Community Bible Church, First Baptist Church Reidsville was the hub from which my life radiated. Grandmother Evelyn had brought her five children up in the church since "cradle roll," a Southern term for the young children of the parish. My mother returned as the prodigal daughter with her own little one in tow: divorced, broke, and starting over at the age of fifty-three.

Thanks to my aunts and uncles, my mother and I had a roof over our heads, a family that supported and loved us, and, most of all, faith. My mother's saving grace was the Baptist church, and she repaid her gratitude with Wednesday and Sunday faithfulness, never once suggesting we stay home so she could rest her tired feet. Her dedication to her Christian faith had not faltered since the days of the High Point Furniture Market.

Where Dana Community Bible Church and Binkley Baptist left off, First Baptist picked up. It became my hot spot—not just because the youth group had a bumper crop of boys but because there was also *nothing* else better, free, or more enticing to do.

China Grill

The cultural shift of the 1990s meant that my mother and I didn't enjoy large, home-centered lunches after church. More women worked, and families ate out after church. Cultural norms no longer urged businesses to close on the sabbath. Staying open proved to be profitable, and consuming seven days per week became the American duty. Resting, after all, does nothing to increase the gross domestic product.

Each Sunday after church, I begged my mother to take me to one of the two exotic culinary establishments in town: Monterrey Mexican or China Grill. We couldn't really afford to eat out, but doing so meant that the hours between worship services and youth group felt shorter, and I longed for the time when we returned to church. After lunch, my mother rested, her body weary from standing all week in the nursing clinic of our county's public health department. Now that I am an adult who works multiple jobs, I don't know how she managed as a single parent. She kept up with our finances and ensured our clothes and dishes stayed clean without a washing machine or dishwasher. Despite being spread thin, she made time to steer me toward a life of faith instead of rebellion. It would have been far easier for her to do otherwise.

My mother took me to church on Sundays and Wednesday evenings for youth events, joining the adult chancel choir so that we could be on the same schedule. She became one of our Baptist church's few female deacons, while also helping establish a church plant for Spanish-speaking members of our community. Like her mother, my mother wanted me to see the importance of living the gospel. For my mother, sabbath was the only relief from the dread of another workweek and a back-breaking list of chores. At church, she found fulfillment, enrichment, and comfort from the demands of our simple but difficult existence.

My Reidsville maternal family also made certain I joined every children's and youth program. By ninth grade, I'd been selected to sit on a search committee for the next associate pastor, who would lead the youth. Pastor John Daugherty ultimately become a mentor, surrogate father, and partner in my own ordination. And though he was a busy clergyman amid cultural change, he too modeled sabbath observance.

John and his wife, Phyllis, had two daughters, one of whom was my age. She and I became close friends. As a result, the Daugherty family gave me access to their private life, and I was privy to what it meant to be clergy outside the church's walls. I saw how exhausting but ultimately rewarding pastoral life could be. Pastor Daugherty, stretched far too thin, cherished sacred Sunday afternoon hours before he had to go back to work. After lunch, he changed from his pressed grey suit into his sweats, napped in his chair, and then transitioned seamlessly back to the hallowed sanctuary every Sunday evening.

Before I could even name it for myself, church taught me that Sundays were different. As I grew older, I stepped out of the rhythm and ritual that Sunday created for worship, food, family, rest, stillness, and solitude. But the lessons were still inside me, all because two sisters had stood their ground, keeping and passing on the sabbath values they'd been taught.

The Young and the Restless

My husband, Fred, and I are no different from America's other privileged residents. We have the basics covered: shelter, food, and health care. We have obligations: jobs, caring for my elderly mother, and keeping up with domestic duties. We toil on computers seven days a week, our electronic devices keeping us constantly "on" and accessible. We hardly have time for spiritual practice, cultivating and maintaining relationships, and truly living—and we don't even have the responsibility of caring for children. Even so, if Fred and I want quiet time each day, we have to rise as early as 4:00 a.m. to get it. After a short chat with God via our devotional practices, prayers, and reading, we retreat to our respective laptops, typing the days (and weekends) away. If we're not careful, each day looks the same; nothing distinguishes the ordinary from the sacred.

Both my maternal and paternal families taught me about the solid marker between the mundane and the auspicious. Until my twenties, Sundays had been sacred days full of wonder. Somehow and somewhere, I'd forgotten about the joy of Sunday school songs and the excitement of youth group crushes—two elements that brought me into the fold of sabbath and lulled me into deeper devotion and practice. As an adult, sabbath no longer held this place in my life. I'd fallen into the trap of using the Lord's Day to catch up. When I was in seminary, I worked Sundays in the parish, but outside that scholarly realm, I reserved the weekends for accomplishing all the projects I hadn't finished during the week.

Since marrying seven years ago, Fred and I began spending Sunday mornings on work projects, running errands in the afternoon, and finishing chores in the evening. Our church attendance is spotty. A few years ago, I began to understand why people don't go to church on Sunday. As a middle and high schooler, I didn't get why anyone would skip the weekly practice that offered new life. I was aware that many folks *had* to work on Sundays, as my own mother had been a weekend nurse. But the sabbath became all the more special when she landed a weekday job, and we could finally attend church together.

Now, in my mid-thirties, even as an ordained clergyperson, I resent how and why someone decided that Sunday at 11:00 a.m. is the most auspicious hour to gather for devotional worship. Once Fred and I drive to church, worship, eat lunch, and attend a church committee meeting or two, the day is nearly gone.

In the days when time *felt* more abundant, a Sunday spent at church made more sense because we were less pressed for breathing room. Globalization, jobs, the 24/7 marketplace, email, heavy workloads, and caregiving all contribute to our feeling suffocated by obligations, and it's no wonder Americans are saying "No thanks" to the one thing they feel can be removed from their lengthy to-do list.

Even when Fred and I do attend worship, I worry about unfinished tasks while I am supposed to be praising God. Under the guise of taking sermon notes, I brain dump my anxiety into scribbles on the bulletin. Liturgies meant to invite me into what Celtic spirituality calls the "thin space" trigger panic of what's been left undone. While the church sings, "I come to the garden alone while the dew is still on the roses," I make a mental note to purchase Mother's Day flowers. When the ministers offer the prayers of the people, I jot down names of those people under my pastoral care whom I need to visit. A sermon on Jesus' acts of social justice fills me with panic, and I think it my duty to start a vegetarian soup kitchen before dusk. By the benediction, I'm totally overwhelmed; I've completely given up on having any meaningful time with God, and a new set of tasks awaits me. Sabbath and church services, therefore, become an unwelcome obligation instead of spiritual fill-up, a time of stress and anxiety instead of a time to reconnect with God.

You Can Lead a Horse to Water

Sabbath is in my muscle memory, springing forth from my deep roots in rural North Carolina and Indiana. I only need to return to the well—and *actually drink* the water.

A few years ago, Fred and I traveled nearly to the equator to find sabbath, isolating ourselves from the world by taking shelter in a remote jungle ashram. At Madhuvan Monastery in Costa Rica, I rode a horse for the first time in my life. She was 105 in horse years, with milky eyes and seasonal allergies. "Sweet Baby Girl" and I spent two hours together, climbing untrodden jungle paths and fearing for our lives.

When Fred and I returned Sweet Baby Girl to her stable, she stopped twenty feet short of the covered barn. We were all hot, tired, and thirsty. The horse's work had been done, and her oasis was in sight. But she wouldn't budge. I pulled her reins, flapped my arms, and jumped around.

"Water! Water!" I shouted, hoping to coax her out of the sun. She stood her nearly one-ton ground. Fred even fetched the bucket and brought it to her snout. She bucked the offering.

"I guess you really can lead a horse to water, but you can't make her drink," I finally said. The Central American sun beat down on us, and the cool water remained untouched at the horse's feet. We were three pilgrims on a path—two human and one equine—each knowing what it's like to need something so basic but to be too stubborn to take it.

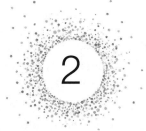

2

SABBATH ROOTS

Stand at the crossroads, and look,
and ask for the ancient paths,
where the good way lies; and walk in it,
and find rest for your souls.

—JEREMIAH 6:16

Fred and I attended our first-ever Jewish Passover Seder in late April 2016. That year, the eight-day observance started Friday night, the beginning of sabbath in the Hebrew tradition. It took place six weeks after I'd lost a Q-tip in my ear. I'd just discontinued the Topomax, but I hadn't yet started the Botox injections for my chronic migraine. Soon, I would examine the *how* of returning to sabbath in a nonstop world. But, first, I needed to know the *why*.

Fred and I arrived at Susan's home just before sundown. Susan is my teaching mentor and an academic director. She had grown up in a Conservative Jewish home in the Bronx in the 1950s. Her family had kept kosher, but she describes herself as both Jewish *and* spiritual, rather than synagogue-going religious. Susan loves all the Jewish traditions: She lights *Shabbat* candles, observes Rosh Hashanah and Yom Kippur, and relishes the joy of Hanukkah. Susan has a long-standing, generous tradition of inviting non-Jewish friends to her family's Passover Seders. Fred and I had been asked to attend for years, but it always conflicted with our interfaith tango of Christianity's Holy Week and the Hindu festival of Gaurapurnima. The 2016 lunar calendar had been kind to us; Passover fell three weeks after our Christian and Hindu holy days. That's how Fred and I found ourselves standing on Susan's front stoop, knocking and ringing the doorbell for at least five minutes before the jovial Passover crowd even noticed us. Curious by the levity of those gathered inside, I didn't yet know how the night would be unlike any other.

Susan and her guests greeted Fred and me with hugs and kisses, and we immediately felt like family. After introductions, thirteen of us sat around a large dining table: three Christians, one Hindu, four unaffiliated, and five Jews—all born and bred, bar and bat mitzvahed. At each place setting sat Susan's special china—the ones she only uses for Passover—and a bowl of salt water, representing the tears the Jews shed in slavery.

Passover commemorates God's deliverance of the enslaved Israelites from Egypt. The *Haggadah* is a read-along liturgy that recounts the story of *Pesach* (Passover), including how it came to be that God convinced Pharaoh to let the people go. The tenth and final plague killed all the firstborn Egyptian sons but spared the Hebrew boys because Moses gave the Jews God's instructions to slaughter a lamb and spread its blood on their door. Seeing the blood of sacrifice, the plague would "pass over" that home.

This particular Passover Seder was especially auspicious because it landed on the sabbath. The evening began with the lighting of the *Shabbat* candles, two thin tapers that slumped over in rebellion—a good metaphor for America's modern resistance to ceasing from its labors. *The Concise Family Seder,* a yellow paperback *Haggadah,* sat atop our plates. Susan's granddaughter, the youngest person in attendance, began by asking the first of Passover's four questions: "How is this night different from all the others?"[1] Susan's son led our continued reading. The Hebrew rolled off his tongue as if a day hadn't passed since his bar mitzvah. During his recitation, the women chastised his swiftness. "Slow down," they urged, wanting to savor each word.

Prior to beginning the reading, Susan and her family had offered Fred and me a primer, including how Passover might be observed in a more traditional Orthodox Jewish setting. Pillows would be part of a stricter evening. Those gathered would recline during the meal, drinking wine and eating slowly, indicative of how those who had enslaved them had lived. At Passover, time and leisure signify privilege and freedom. The very act of spending an entire day (or evening) feasting and relaxing demonstrates liberation from the bonds of slavery. The enslaved are no longer entrapped by another person, institution, culture, or economy. The pace of the Passover Seder, with its wine-pouring and mindful chewing of each bite, celebrates a freedom I did not yet understand.

Among the several bottles of wine for the guests, a six-dollar glass bottle of Manischevitz sat untouched. "It tastes like cough syrup," the other guests warned, describing the kosher libation. Fred and I don't drink, but we insisted on living into the full experience of Passover, including its customary beverage. Tiny glasses were retrieved for us, and everyone laughed about the Gentiles insisting on tradition.

Each guest took turns reading from the *Haggadah*. Fred and I fumbled over transliterated Hebrew. The story unfolded, and we were drawn further into its theme: "How is this night different from all the others?" At the center of the table, the *afikomen*, a broken piece of *matzah* (unleavened bread), was placed in a silk bag on a Seder platter. Later, the final piece was hidden, and Susan's granddaughter retrieved it in exchange for the cash in her father's wallet, as is tradition.

The Seder guests laughed and drank and choked on Susan's extra hot horseradish (symbolizing the bitterness of slavery). We learned that everything in Judaism has meaning, including Passover's Seder ingredients. We moved through each ritual as if time and freedom were plentiful. Four hours later, just before 11:00 p.m., we poured a cup of wine for the prophet Elijah, opened Susan's front door, and symbolically invited him in as the final act of hospitality. On that sabbath night, we reclined in sacred time, catching a glimpse of eternity. Ceasing was sweeter than any work imaginable.

Fred and I felt honored to be invited into a mystical night of both Passover *and* sabbath. We put down the smartphones that entrap us. We shifted our posture, reclining and aligning ourselves with God, scripture, and community. We cut the cord of unnecessary urgency and simply embraced the present. It had been a long time since I'd let holy mystery transcend daily chaos.

As Fred and I climbed into bed after midnight, I realized that for the first time in weeks I didn't have a migraine. "Why aren't we celebrating the gift of sabbath freedom each week?" I asked him.

"That Don't Fit My Schedule."

The Christmas after Fred and I were engaged, my mother and I spent the holiday with Fred's paternal family: his parents; his grandparents, Granny and Granddad; and Granddad's sister, Great-Aunt Gloria, whom we call Aunt Glo. The two sisters-in-law, Granny and Aunt Glo, could not be more different. Aunt Glo is a devout vegetarian and Seventh-day Adventist (SDA); Granny was a Texas-born Christian who worshiped at the altar of "Dancing with the Stars."

The Christmas gathering took place at Fred's family lake house, which is not far from Concord Mills mall, a 1.4-million-square-foot heaven (or hell, depending upon whom you ask) of consumerism. The shopping monstrosity is a trophy to capitalism and a death trap for impulsive shoppers. The day after Christmas, Granny wanted the entire family to take a field trip there. But it was Saturday, and Aunt Glo and her fellow Seventh-day Adventists follow Jesus' life and guidelines as closely as possible, including the keeping of a Hebrew Saturday sabbath. This means that Aunt Glo and SDAs do not buy, spend, or labor on Saturday. They view sabbath as a gift that will help herald the Second Coming. In keeping with following Jesus, they refrain from any worldly activities on the Lord's Day. Instead of shopping, Aunt Glo keeps the sabbath by resting, praying, singing hymns, and taking part in Bible study. She reads the *Adventist Review* and attends Sabbath school and church services. For the SDA community, the sabbath also often includes outdoor walks and spreading cheer at local nursing homes.[2, 3]

Granny was upset that Aunt Glo wouldn't join the family at the mall. Granddad had been raised in the same tradition as his sister, but he was not an adherent.

"Why didn't you become a Seventh-day Adventist when you married Granddad?" I asked Granny over breakfast.

"That don't fit my schedule," she cackled, referring to the Saturday sabbaths while taking a drag off her generic cigarette.

I understood Granny's resistance but also respected Aunt Glo's persistence. Sabbath practices, whether observed on a Saturday, Sunday, or Tuesday, are difficult to maintain amid modern cultural expectations. Even the ancient Hebrew people faced sabbath obstacles thousands of years ago while enslaved and in exile. Despite turmoil and persecution, the Jews had managed to make it work for millennia, embracing the gift given through Creation. Today, however, while no American laws forbid observing sabbath, only a handful of Abrahamic traditions keep strict sabbaths: Judaism, Seventh-day Adventism, and the Church of Jesus Christ of Latter-Day Saints (Mormonism). Most Christians I know—myself included—echo Granny's authentic sentiment: "That don't fit my schedule."

Ancient Roots, Modern Medicine

America is good at making the old new again. Yoga, though well over three thousand years old and indigenous to India and Hinduism, is all the rage in the United States. Studios of all yoga persuasions can be found in nearly every medium-to-large-sized town. *Meditation* and *mindfulness*, also ancient practices original to India and Buddhism, are buzzwords now embedded in our twenty-first-century culture. Yoga, meditation, and mindfulness seem shiny and innovative—but they are spiritual practices with long track records. What makes them appear novel is how they continue to soothe the chaos of modernity. If turning to ancient practices to solve new problems is cool, the Christian church should take a page from its Jewish roots.

Old Testament scholar Walter Brueggemann, who describes sabbath as a "distinctly Jewish art form," writes that Christians should have no problem dusting off an ancient Hebrew spiritual practice to cure modern woes.[4] Christians may find this suggestion prickly; they tend to neglect Jesus' Jewishness and forget that a strict sabbath observance was central to his faith and life. For Jews of all types (Hasidic, Orthodox, Conservative, Reform, Reconstructionist, and Secular), sabbath is important. Regardless of stage of life or level of interest in religious practice, sabbath is accessible to Jews each week. It is a gift that can be opened or rejected.

Go Within or Go Without

I met Judith Harrow at Susan Mitzner's Passover Seder. She read my first book, and we share a first name. We only spoke briefly at the Seder, but later I emailed her for advice on how to reignite my own sabbath practice.

Judy says her life is based on Jewish values. *Shabbat,* she wrote me, should be used as a time to turn inward, building a sanctuary in the heart and mind to escape the 24/7, "nattering" society. For her, sabbath provides space to "pause in order to discover, consider, and implement ways of being in the world that add meaning."[5]

The seventh day, then, is a weekly glimpse into the mystery that is God. Judy offers that, amid our busyness, *Shabbat* helps us see how our lives are "immersed in ordinary holiness" that otherwise would go unnoticed. Like that Passover night, I learned that sabbath is a gift of slowing down; giving thanks; offering praise; and enjoying the blessings of friends, family, community, and the bounty of our lush, green earth. Judy believes that *Shabbat* can mend the broken and aching parts of our lives while also cultivating a more fulfilling life. She tells me that once we step out of our actual or metaphorical sabbath sanctuaries, we are more prepared and inclined to participate fully in *tikkun olam*—or "repairing the world."

Judy's words struck me as exactly how Jesus viewed the sabbath: a day to keep holy, a day to acknowledge our blessings, and a day to repair. Jesus observed not only the inner work of sabbath (studying in the temple and praying) but also the outer work (feeding the hungry and healing the sick). He saw the world's needs because he was rooted in God through scripture and filled with the Holy Spirit.

I, on the other hand, can't even see the very gift that lies before me. My ego fuels my drivenness and ultimately wreaks havoc on my health. Susan's Passover Seder made me realize I need *both* parts of what Judy is suggesting: the sanctuary of meditation and prayer *and* the participation in *tikkun olam*. These practices, she tells me, are the antidote for a host of self-centered, twenty-first-century ills.

When Christians use sabbath time to confront our "golden calves"—ego, unpiousness, selfishness, envy, greed, lust, and pride—we get to join our Jewish brothers and sisters in a practice that holds the power to change the world. Christians can rediscover their connection with Judaism as it relates to sabbath by returning to these ancient Hebrew ways, just as we are quick to try yoga or meditation.

Set Apart

Millennia ago, God commanded the Israelites to keep the sabbath day holy. Following this decree set the Israelites apart from their neighbors. We first learn of sabbath in the six-day Creation narrative found in Genesis. It pops up again in the Israelites' enslavement and desert wandering and is finally cemented in the law given to Moses through the Ten Commandments on Mount Sinai. Ceasing from labor after six days of work is woven thoughtfully and repeatedly into the fabric of Judaism.

Though seemingly legalistic to Christians, Jewish sabbath rules have a deeper purpose than telling us to stop our work. To *remember* the sabbath and to *keep it holy* is to honor both creation itself and the Creator who saved the Jews from endless toil under Pharaoh. For Jews, sabbath is the gift of time God granted to a shackled people who did not own their own time. The most radical, rebellious thing enslaved persons can do with their time is to use it for awe—not production. Like the Passover Seder, stopping to recline in mystery is antithetical to the master's bottom line.

In the modern Jewish tradition, this ancient gift of time is still observed as a day of freedom from the thirty-nine categories of work—everything from plowing, sowing, ripping, cooking, wringing a wet garment, tying a knot, building, demolishing, to carrying something from the public to the private domain or vice versa.[6] Instead, sabbath is time spent with God in prayer and study and time spent with family and community. No money is exchanged or touched on the sabbath. No one travels, takes part in goal-oriented self-improvement, tackles difficult issues or problems, or produces, creates, or destroys anything.[7] Instead, the day offers a glimpse into eternity, much like the Passover Seder at Susan's where we ate, drank, studied, and remembered.

In his classic book *The Sabbath: Its Meaning for Modern Man,* Rabbi Abraham Joshua Heschel calls Judaism's sabbath the "palace in time."[8] For Heschel, both historically and in today's culture, time is the ultimate form of wealth in human society.[9] Time is humanity's most valuable nonrenewable resource, so reclaiming twenty-four hours per week rebels against the dominant culture of production and consumption. To set an entire day aside for nothing but spiritual gain is to be wealthy in a way that transcends bank accounts. But time spent in spiritual introspection is the enemy of our economic machine. In western, consumer-driven countries like the United States, the more people work, the more they contribute to economic growth. Sabbath activities like rest, shared meals, worship, prayer, study, and making love (as is decreed by Jewish law) do nothing to contribute to a capitalist society.[10]

When we fail to observe this God-given gift of sabbath time, we have embezzled our own lives.[11] The cost, in turn, is devastating. We fritter away our time, stealing from ourselves the gifts of meaning, awakening, and deepening our relationship with the Divine and others. Heschel writes that the self that emerges from a day of sabbath is a changed one. Sabbath should be the one-seventh of our lives that shapes the remaining six-sevenths.

Doing Justice, Loving Mercy, Walking Humbly— Especially on the Sabbath

Twenty-first-century rabbis share Heschel's concerns over diminishing sabbath observation, a decline Heschel experienced in the 1950s. Rabbi

Larry Bach calls sabbath "our best spiritual technology," and yet, he shepherds a flock that faces unique societal pressures and challenges to keeping the seventh day holy.[12]

Susan introduced me to Rabbi Bach the year before her Passover Seder. Bach is a vibrant, young clergyman who shepherds Judea Reform Congregation in Durham, North Carolina. In his temple, he reminds his congregants that God has called them to observe the six-and-one rhythm of creation and rest that is contrary to our modern pace. Bach describes the sabbath parameters in this way: In the first Creation story, God creates everything in six days, but the act of creating lasts seven days. What is fashioned on the last day is *menuchah*—or "sacred rest." *Sabbath*, or *Shabbat* in Hebrew, literally means "to stop or cease" in order to observe *menuchah*. *Menuchah*, therefore, becomes not only a ceasing from our labors but also a lifting up and a celebration of everything in God's creation.[13]

Rabbi Bach makes his beliefs clear to his community: *Menuchah* is not resting so that we may be productive in the material sense of the word; it is not a goal-oriented respite. In the Jewish practice, *Shabbat* is distinct from ordinary, everyday time. Jewish law says that nothing should be created or destroyed on the sabbath. Those observing the sabbath should not gain anything materially; they should not add to the economy. But they should grow spiritually. We partake in *menuchah* in order to be participants in the awe and joy of God's creation.

The *Talmud*, which is rabbinic commentary on the *Torah* (the first five books of the Old Testament), shares this dichotomy of material and spiritual time. Rabbi Bach recounts the following story: A rabbi walks prayerfully along his property on the sabbath and comes upon a broken fence. He makes a mental note to repair the fence when the sabbath is over. As soon as he has added the task to his to-do list, he realizes he's broken the sabbath. The rabbi then decides that the fence can never be fixed, even after *Shabbat* has concluded. It must remain in its current state of disrepair in order to remind him of the importance of honoring the very delineation of ordinary and sacred time. Heschel echoes this sentiment in *The Sabbath*:

The meaning of the Sabbath is to celebrate time rather than space. Six days a week we live under the tyranny of things of space; on the Sabbath we try to become attuned to *holiness in time*. It is a day on which we are called upon to share in what is eternal in time, to turn from the results of creation to the mystery of creation.[14]

Rabbi Bach and his clergy contemporaries face a challenge in implementing Heschel's wisdom. How does a well-educated, progressive, social-justice-minded faith leader shepherd a twenty-first-century flock addicted to smartphones and social media? How can rabbis and ministers convince community members to rest when they wrestle with society's pressure to be "on" at all times?

Bach's ideal sabbath for himself and his synagogue members includes prayer, study, and shared meals. But he offers a refreshingly modern exegesis for those reconciling scripture's commandment with the need to be active on Saturdays and Sundays. While Bach believes strongly that sabbath is about refraining from our own ordinary work, he believes we can do God's work instead. Sabbath, he explains, doesn't have to be restricted to only rest, solitary activities, or closed gatherings that only include his congregants. He values activism on the seventh day. Bach encourages his Reform Judaism congregation to host public gatherings on Saturday that build community or *tikkun olam*—furthering God's work in repairing the world and bringing about justice for the oppressed.

Persons who crave authenticity and action will appreciate this modern spin on the ancient practice. Bach's intention for his congregants echoes the Micah 6:8 banner carried by many Christian churches, save one edit: "To do justice, and to love kindness, and to walk humbly with your God—*especially on the sabbath.*"

Bach insists that *doing something* on the sabbath can be spiritually fulfilling if it is balanced with devotion, study, and prayer to keep the intention in focus. Given Bach's exegesis, a full sabbath may include solitude (rest and prayer), illumination and devotion (worship), and unification (community and service). This schedule follows a natural progression of turning inward, away from the world, to commune with God and then returning to the world as a spiritually different person.

Intention, Not Hours

At the beginning of a traditional Jewish Friday night sabbath, two candles are lit sixteen minutes before the sun crosses the horizon. Many sabbath-observing Jews remain in *Shabbat* mode until full darkness on Saturday night—or when three stars are visible in the sky. Among the breadth of Judaism, much like the variety of Christian denominations, people hold differing opinions as to what constitutes this twenty-four-to-twenty-five-hour period of time. The more orthodox a Jew is in his or her practice, the more time he or she adds to cushion the beginning and ending of the sabbath observance (forty to eighty minutes) to ensure he or she has not transgressed the sabbath day.

For Rabbi Bach and many other Jewish teachers, the spirit of the practice creates *Shabbat*, not necessarily the number of hours spent observing it. No matter what a person "does" from Friday evening to Saturday at sundown, sabbath rules insist that actions should be done with the intention of Exodus 20:8—that is, to remember the sabbath and *lekadsho* ("to sanctify it"). Such sanctifying activities include resting, delighting, seeking, and deepening a spiritual practice. But Bach admits that even with his wide definition of sabbath, not all his temple members participate.

Those who do observe sabbath can choose from any number of activities. Throughout the traditional twenty-four hours of ceasing, Bach finds that his congregants may engage in one or two aspects of sabbath but not necessarily keep the entire period of sabbath, which is the more orthodox understanding of the day. Some come to temple services on Friday evening; others bake two loaves of *challah* (a bread that serves as a reminder of the double portion of manna the Israelites received in the desert the day before the sabbath) and light candles at home. Some families cook a special dinner. Other members of Bach's community are faithful Saturday observers, attending services and Talmud studies.

Ritual and Ethics

After the Hebrew people were freed from slavery, wandered in the desert, and received the Ten Commandments from Moses, their lives became properly ordered into two categories of dos and don'ts: rituals (things they must do to keep them connected to God) and ethics (things they must do to remain peacefully connected to others). Observing the sabbath is number four among the list of ten and on the ritual side of the law.

Rabbi Bach says the ritual and ethical sides of the Ten Commandments can inform each other. He explains that one *midrash* (Rabbinical interpretation) suggests that the commandments may be read across, not down. This practice pairs each ritual with an ethic. Honoring the sabbath (number four) corresponds with not lying (number nine). Therefore, not observing sabbath could be considered bearing false witness—or lying—against ourselves and our neighbors. In this way, not accepting the gift of *menuchah* is to deny who and whose we are.

Rabbi Bach finds that his synagogue members are more motivated by sabbath encouragement and flexibility than by harsh legalism. Because sabbath falls on the ritual side of the Decalogue, it's less black-and-white than ethics. His congregants more easily digest his urges not to murder one another than they do his insistence that they observe a full twenty-four hours of rest, study, and community—no matter the circumstances. But Bach also challenges the assumption that his congregants should view sabbath as merely a ritual obligation. For Bach, *Shabbat* is where ritual meets ethics: Nurturing ourselves and affirming our connection and dependence upon God helps us keep the remaining nine commandments.

Rabbi Bach knows not everyone can or will jump on the sabbath bandwagon. Interest, time, jobs, and family responsibilities limit or inhibit our ability to keep a full day of rest. The freedom of rest in modern (and in ancient) times often resides with the privileged few. No matter our circumstances or ability to keep sabbath—whether we would rather be doing something else or *have* to be doing something else—Rabbi Bach encourages us to grab moments of sabbath however our schedules will yield and to see the practice as worthwhile.

Heschel might disagree with the contemporary sabbath-keeping method of embracing *menuchah* as our lives permit. He wrote *The Sabbath* in 1951 in part as a polemic against Conservative Judaism's decision to allow driving on Saturdays. *The Sabbath* has become the most well-read book on sabbath among Jews and Gentiles alike. Though Heschel's work was prophetic, Bach notes that Heschel was writing in an era when no one had the kind of demands on his or her time that we have today. Heschel could mark a clear delineation between his work and his rest.

Though Bach thinks Heschel would still be as countercultural today as he was nearly seven decades ago, he knows we don't necessarily have the luxury of 1950s-paced culture, society, and work demands. Times (and culture) have changed. If Heschel wrote the updated edition of *The Sabbath* today, he'd have a lot more to contend with than driving. But Bach believes that Heschel would remain just as steadfast in preserving the entirety of the practice. Even amid the information and social media age, Heschel would tell us not to let go of something as precious as sabbath just because we feel economic or societal pressure.

Just as Rabbi Bach tries to honor the strict lines Heschel and others before him sought to keep, he knows he must be a flexible faith leader. He and his staff model the intentionality they wish for their congregation. They set a sabbath example by ceasing from their temple administrative work on Friday afternoons to create a welcoming mood for Friday night service attendees. When their congregants arrive that evening, exhausted from the workweek, the temple staff ensures that they are informed and transformed by the mystical space that transcends time.

But Bach's synagogue has had to make tough compromises to balance *Shabbat* with reality. When the temple needed a new roof, the general contractor wanted his team to work late Friday afternoons and all-day Saturday to complete the project. Confronted with a decision of building needs versus theology, Bach led the congregation through a discernment process, drawing respectful but firm lines. Without imposing their Jewish beliefs on the beliefs held by the roofers, the congregants agreed that the work could be done until 4:00 p.m. on Friday but then must cease during services and study until midafternoon on Saturday.

No matter how his flock chooses to keep sabbath, Bach teaches its power and possibilities. Bach thinks Christians could also seize the opportunity to keep sabbath and be prophetic. By revisiting Jesus' Jewish roots, Christians can honor the time and energy that went into perfecting the Hebrew sabbath over the past three thousand years while also continuing to explore the sabbath through a christological lens. Though Paul's conversion and his aversion to Jewish law meant that Jesus' followers have historically shied away from a twenty-four-hour Hebrew sabbath, Christians could benefit from engaging in a Torah refresher. Embracing the full day—or at least a more formal observance of sabbath—is an opportunity to reappraise the New Testament writer's rejection of what he considered the legalistic Hebrew texts.

Friday night and Saturday sabbath services have retained their popularity in Judaism, even among those who label themselves secular Jews. Bach suspects the enduring popularity of sabbath stems from the power of repetition. The Hebrew community has observed this weekly ritual globally for thousands of years, creating a powerful foundation of both habit and solidarity. Bach also thinks Judaism is good at leaning into its very best thing: the rhythm of doing and pausing, of six and one, a true relief from our culture's 24/7 rhythm. Given the steady decline of the American church, Christians should take note.

Jesus was a faithful—though rebellious—sabbath observer. When the sabbath arrived, he marked the day with many different kinds of practices, even amid disdain. He sought solitude, he taught, he healed, he advocated for the marginalized, and he admonished. Christians can revisit how Jesus spent sabbath by considering Bach's theological construct of doing *God's* work on the sabbath (just as Jesus did), not our own. A Christian observance of a Hebrew-rooted sabbath creates a *Shabbat* that is both true to Christianity and respectful of Judaism.

Sabbath also can serve as a point of unification among the Abrahamic faiths. When confronted with prejudices, misunderstandings, and cultural and societal pressures, Jews and Christians can resist the idea that we always must be doing, working, and buying. Though not necessarily categorized as sabbath, Muslims also observe communal prayer time on Fridays (called *Al-Jumuah*). The Islamic community gathers to pray *together* and listen to a brief sermon. In predominately Muslim countries and neighborhoods—much like Jewish neighborhoods—stores close, workers leave offices, and the faithful gather together.[15] If all American Abrahamic practitioners (Jews, Christians, and Muslims) resolved to truly stop—whether on Friday afternoon, on Saturday, or on Sunday—we would start a mass movement. We'd be more focused on the things that truly matter, and our spiritual practice could bear much witness.

Sabbath Accountability

In Exodus, the Israelites come to face-to-face with sabbath accountability. Its arrival is expressed first in Creation and then again in the stories of the Israelites' enslavement and wilderness exile. Observing *Shabbat* in the desert means total reliance upon God, who provides a double portion of manna on the sixth day to last through the sabbath. The Jews are forbidden from taking a double portion on any day but the sixth, as manna rots quickly. But food gathered just before the sabbath doesn't spoil. God keeps the Israelites free from work on the sabbath because the Lord provides everything they need.

God is so insistent that the Israelites cease from their labors that God punishes those who disobey. In the book of Numbers, the Israelites come upon a man chopping wood in the forest on the sabbath. Moses and Aaron ask God what to do. God says that the man must be stoned to death, and this decision shocks the entire camp. The consequences feel too steep for modern hearts, but God is keen on teaching the Hebrews a lesson in dependence, accountability, and solidarity. If God allows one person to labor on the sabbath, others will feel that they cannot afford to cease from their own work.[16]

To Observe or Not to Observe

Judith Shulevitz, author of *The Sabbath World: Glimpses of a Different Order of Time*, reminds us that early and modern Christians had and have mixed feelings about Judaism's practices. The apostle Paul, a Jew-turned-Christian missionary, was the first in line to rail against Jewish law to Jesus' followers. Would Jesus have wanted Christians to observe sabbath? If so, how? Or, as Shulevitz writes, was sabbath just "too *Jewish*, a discardable artifact of Jewish 'chosenness,' antithetical to the spirit of the new universal religion?"[17]

Christians, particularly Protestants, fear revisiting the Hebrew roots of sabbath and Jesus' Jewishness. This aversion stems from Jesus' fulfillment of the law (Matthew 5:17) and Paul's emphasis on the New Covenant, such that he no longer felt a need for Christians to be tied to Judaism. Still, approaching sabbath with a posture of humility and growth would mean asking tough questions, such as, Why do Christians refuse the very gift rooted in Creation that would actually make their faith stronger? For his part, Bach believes that Jews should be gracious and hospitable in encouraging Christians to share in the practice as they will. He even offers a place to start: "Turn off your phone."

This simple wisdom comes from a teacher with a vast canon of scripture and commentary at his fingertips. Driving was among Heschel's 1950s sabbath challenges, but technology that fits in the palm of our hands is ours. Being plugged in keeps us tethered to that which embezzles time meant for ourselves, God, and community. Bach believes becoming unyoked from that which binds us is a good place to start.

Jesus and the Sabbath

The practice of sabbath becomes written in stone when Moses shares the Ten Commandments given from God. Centuries after the Exodus, Jesus arrives and shakes things up. He is deeply rooted in Judaism, born of a Hebrew family and raised to study the Torah, but he tests the limits of the religious establishment. Jesus knows the sabbath laws well—their boundaries, communal ties, economic impacts, and meaning for a people once enslaved and who wandered for forty years to learn the tough lesson of dependence on God and one another. But Jesus' ministry is about immediacy.

The Gospel of Mark, likely crafted around 68–73 CE is short, full of verbs, and contains the word *immediately* (the Greek word *euthys*) forty-one of the fifty-one times it's used in the New Testament. Mark's Gospel, the first canonical Gospel that was written, throws us into Jesus' story at his baptism when the Spirit *immediately* descends upon him. Then he *immediately* goes to the wilderness for spiritual boot camp.[18]

The Gospel of Mark moves at top speed, and when Jesus returns from wilderness solitude and Satan's testing, he drives the demon out of a man in Capernaum on the sabbath. Bystanders stand in awe of the miracle; the Pharisees, however, are frustrated with Jesus' disregard for sabbath laws of no "work" (including healing) on the seventh day.[19] The Gospel of Mark is full of stories like this one: bold and quick, with Jesus utilizing his author-ity from God.[20] Despite continued opposition, Jesus' observation of sabbath intrigues his followers. He continues to heal on the sabbath—he and his students even gather grain to feed the hungry.[21]

Readers of Mark learn quickly that Jesus values the sabbath, but he also seeks to redefine it. He sums up his sabbath rebellion against legalism for his followers by saying, "The Son of Man is lord even of the sabbath" (Mark 2:28). Jesus consistently breaks the rules and seeks a *relational* sabbath: He touches people; he heals; he redeems; he teaches—all from a powerful, mystical force beyond his humanity.

When Jesus cures the bent-over woman on the sabbath, much to the annoyance of the synagogue leader, Jesus is told healing should be done on the other six days. Jesus refutes this argument, calling the leader a hypocrite, because he unties his animals to give them water on the sev-enth day. The woman, Jesus says, deserves the same relief from what has ailed her. (See Luke 13:10-17.)

Over and over, Jesus "labors" on the sabbath, doing good deeds that the temple priests see as "working." He rationalizes his actions, saying, "My Father is still working, and I also am working" (John 5:17). From the start of his ministry on the sabbath to his acts of service, Jesus is the rule-breaking "lord of the sabbath." But he doesn't indulge in luxury, for-get God, or strive to achieve goals in the ordinary sense. He "works" for justice, love, and mercy on the sabbath, balancing teaching large crowds with taking time away by himself for introspection.

Loner Jesus

Just as often as Jesus teaches and heals, he disappears. In *Sabbath: Finding Rest, Renewal, and Delight in Our Busy Lives*, Wayne Muller writes that Jesus doesn't wait for everyone to be healed before he seeks time by himself. When Jesus feels his service is done for the time being, he goes to a "lonely" place for solitude, prayer, and a spiritual fill-up. (See Matthew 14:23; Luke 5:15-16; Mark 1:32-33, 35-36.) Jesus' sabbath demonstrates a rhythm of love and contemplation, being in community and in solitude.[22] His disciples learn a new way of looking at what will eventually evolve into the Christian sabbath—or "The Lord's Day."

It's important to note that Jesus insists on keeping the Hebrew mandate of not working for material gain on the sabbath. Like the wandering Jews, he trusts that God will provide. Just as the Israelites were taught to collect a double portion of manna in preparation for *Shabbat*, Jesus does not fret over where he will sleep or what he will eat. He instructs his students to do likewise: "Consider the lilies, how they grow: they neither toil nor spin" (Luke 12:27).

Early Christian Sabbath Practices

In the short three-year ministry that culminates in his death and resurrection, Jesus reshapes sabbath, even by the day of the week. Crucified on a Friday, he appears to Mary Magdalene on a Sunday, the first day of the week according to the Roman calendar. He continues to pop up on Sundays, sharing supper with friends and explaining the fulfillment of the scriptures.

Jesus' actions lead his followers to embrace sabbath as the "eighth day," or first day of the week, rather than the traditional Jewish *Shabbat* on the seventh day (Saturday), or last day of Creation. This eighth-day (or the first day of the Roman week) observance denotes a shift from a Hebrew

sabbath to what ultimately becomes a Christian sabbath. The weekly
cycle observed in Christianity connects the work of Creation to the New
Covenant in Christ. Generations after Jesus' ministry on earth, Sunday-
sabbaths evolve into weekly "little Easter" remembrances, commemorat-
ing the death and resurrection of the beloved teacher and Savior.[23] With
Paul's help, early Christians continue to distinguish themselves from
Judaism and the law, eager to embrace this "eighth day" theology as the
"Lord's Day," or the metamorphosis into the new innovation of sabbath.[24]

While sabbath remains tied to the greater significance of the Genesis
Creation narrative and the economic justice of Jubilee (the year at the end
of a seven-year cycle when all enslaved persons are freed, debts are forgiven,
and land is returned to its former owner), in the decades following Jesus'
death and resurrection, it takes on an additional theological layer: an escha-
tological one, or "having to do with the end."[25] For Christians, the messianic
prophecies have been fulfilled. And because the Messiah has come—and
will come again soon—Christ's followers take an End-Times view of weekly
living, making the "Lord's Day" observances all the more urgent. Even Paul
believed that Jesus would return within Paul's own lifetime.[26]

Early Christian scripture was compiled with this idea in mind: The
end is near; repent and be saved. Sunday sabbath observances serve as a
reminder of this. Though Jesus does not return as expected in the years
following his resurrection, the early Christian church is born amid a culture of hope and anticipation, celebrated each Sunday. When Jesus does
not return right away, the sabbath continues to unfurl, influenced by
church writers and theologians. Paul's opposition to "Judaizing" Christianity significantly influences its early formation. Paul isn't convinced that
Christians need to practice Jewish law in order to be a part of the New
Covenant established in Christ. But many Jewish and Gentile Christians
observe sabbath anyway, taking cues from Jesus' inherent Jewishness.
They demonstrate an unwillingness to leave a known order of things in
favor for unmapped religious territory.[27]

Paul's insistence on an End-Times narrative rejects a need for the law.
The apostle writes that Jesus came to erase lines, not draw them. All are
one; there is neither Jew nor Greek, free nor enslaved, male nor female.

(See Galatians 3:28.) While Christian sabbath practices remove Gentiles from the yoke of the Jewish law, this new way isn't commanded by scripture, as the Hebrew observance had been. There is no definitive scripture outline for precisely how Christians should practice sabbath.

Even with no standard Sunday liturgy from Jesus or texts about how Christians should observe sabbath, rituals began to take shape by the early second century. Christians gathered in private homes on Sundays for a sabbath of fasting, breaking fasts with shared meals, and storytelling. Early church father Ignatius, the Bishop of Antioch, and second-century defender of the faith Justin Martyr both alluded to Christian Sunday sabbath practices in their writings. As early as 250 CE, Christian author Tertullian writes that kneeling and communal prayer had infiltrated Christian gatherings. Fourth century writings from the *Apostolic Constitutions* state that the sabbath was kept weekly among Christians as a festival honoring new creation through Christ's resurrection.[28]

By 321 CE, Christianity's most popular convert, Roman Emperor Constantine, made Christianity and its practices the norm, including observing a Sunday sabbath. As a new Christian, he banned official business and manufacturing on Sunday, an indicator that eighth-day sabbath practices were widespread by that time.[29] Constantine's move wasn't considered too outrageous to the Empire or to Roman pagans. Solar Monotheism, or worshiping of the Sol Invictus deity, also took place on Sundays, which worked in Constantine's favor. In 380 CE, six decades after the Emperor made Sunday the Empire's mandated day of rest, the Roman Empire declared Christianity its official religion.[30]

Constantine's advocacy paved the way for Christians to move from private sabbath observation in homes to public buildings—and with this change, the Christian church found an official position in the public square. Its formation continued to evolve through councils, the Great Schism of 1054, and, ultimately, the Protestant Reformation, which began in 1517. The Reformation and advent of the printing press placed scripture directly into the hands of laypeople. As texts were translated into languages other than Latin, Christians began to interpret God's Word in light of their own cultures and customs.[31] This opened the floodgates for the inception of Christian denominations, and soon Christians disagreed on the nuances of scripture and Jesus' teachings, including sabbath observances.

Discrepancies on how and when to observe sabbath continued well into the development of North American Protestantism. Colonists arrived in the Americas with their Puritan work ethic and resistance to idleness. Sabbath, then, over millennia, transformed from its Hebrew roots of a day of wonder, rest, and joy, to a day of dutiful obligation: worship and austerities commemorating Jesus' ministry, death, and resurrection.[32]

Puritans believed that when Paul called for Christians to give alms to the poor on Sunday in First Corinthians, sabbath was officially transferred to that day. American Puritans were fervent in their observance of the fourth commandment, believing that sabbath practices purified the sins of the week. Their church services were tedious, including long sermons in buildings that had no heat and pews without backs.[33] For the Puritans, sabbath was a far cry from *menuchah*—the reclining freedom of the Passover Seder.

Puritans' sabbath restrictions rubbed off on the budding American culture. Nearly everyone living today has heard the term *blue law* (eighteenth-century slang for moral laws said to have been written on blue paper); the Puritans shaped our early society more than we realize.[34]

Eventually, resistance to Puritan morality ushered in an era in favor of freedom and individual pleasures. Because the Puritans sacrificed *menuchah* in lieu of legalistic piety, many would-be sabbath practitioners lost interest. Additionally, when industrialization connected economies and communities, social norms shifted. Leisure became popular, and it turns out many humans would rather spend time dabbling in the arts and culture than going to church. The church's stronghold on Sundays eroded, and sabbath practices no longer served as a societal default.

Puritanism yielded to a looser Sunday of personal and social development. The American weekend began to symbolize reconnecting with the parts of ourselves we could not access while working. Exercising, entertainment, walks, and time in nature offer a sabbath based on psychological benefits and human welfare.[35]

In 1938, the Fair Labor Standards Act established the forty-hour workweek and eight-hour shifts, reinforcing the modern theme that Sunday is for rest and self-improvement. But blue laws that prevented American businesses from being open or serving alcohol on Sundays persisted until the twenty-first century. Judith Shulevitz suggests that the 1960s and 1970s feminist movement also led to a broader cultural shift in Sundays and sabbath. When women began working more outside the home, they had less time to shop during the workweek. The rate of divorce increased, and single-parent households were forced to complete domestic duties, including shopping, on weekends.[36]

Back to Basics

From the Exodus to the Gospel of Mark, from Constantine to the Puritans, sabbath has evolved within the Judeo-Christian narrative. Regardless of where the church landed on sabbath mandates (Do we observe on Saturday or Sunday? What does sabbath really symbolize?), many people of faith—even the most pious—have lost their sense of what it means to observe sabbath.

Author Donna Schaper writes that when people are asked today how they rest each week, they don't respond with, "Oh, I go to church." Church is seen as an obligation, not a balm. Schaper says that people now seek sabbath outside of religion.[37] While valuing the individual over the authority of the church can be empowering, it often comes at the cost of community and accountability. The most important aspect of "authority" when it comes to sabbath is not the individual's or church's idea of what sabbath should or shouldn't be. The essential ingredient of sabbath is making it holy by making it God's.

Modern Christians have an opportunity to empathize with the challenges the Jews have encountered in observing sabbath in a culture that is neither conducive to nor supportive of taking a full day to connect with the Creator, ourselves, and one another. But even a rigorous review of scripture and Judeo-Christian history doesn't solve the major obstacle against sabbatarianism: How do we begin to observe a day that is antithetical to culture, the economy, smartphones, email, work expectations, and retail? How do American Christians, who are leaving the church in droves, return to sabbath?

Perhaps we should seek the wisdom of our Jewish brothers and sisters who—amid persecution, secularism, and minority views—remain committed and countercultural, drawing strict lines around their sabbath observance. The time is ripe for Christianity to revisit the very heart of sabbath practice in order to create a more meaningful weekly observance of who we are and whose we are. The time is ripe for me too.

3

SABBATH, CULTURE, AND THE ECONOMY OF FRENZY

Teach us to number our days, that we may apply our hearts unto wisdom.
—PSALM 90:12, KJV

How we spend our days is, of course, how we spend our lives.
—ANNIE DILLARD, THE WRITING LIFE

At the start of each college class I teach, I share the following announcement, which I adapted from the airline industry's pre-airplane mode spiel: "Please put away all electronic devices. Anything with an on-off switch must be stowed for the duration of our flight."

Students either think I'm hilarious or crazy, but my message is clear. Unless students need learning accommodations, their phones, tablets, and laptops have no place in my classroom. My reasons are twofold: (1) I want my students to give the curriculum and their classmates their undivided attention, and (2) I'm far too nosy to allow them to be engrossed in something to which I'm not privy. What my students don't know is that when their phones are out, I'm dying to see what's got them so entranced. I'm the one who is distracted. *What does that text say?* I ask myself. *Are those tweets grammatically correct? How does Snapchat work anyway?*

Friends, IRL

Once, while cell-phone spying, I noticed a young woman watching an episode of *Friends*. She wasn't a day older than eighteen, and though she didn't know it, she was part of a growing sample set I was collecting that confirmed an article I'd just read. Adolescents are obsessed with the show *Friends*. The sitcom that dominated America from 1994 to 2004 (for a total of 236 episodes or eighty-eight hours) is considered cool to viewers who weren't even born at the show's debut.[1]

Friends encompassed an era: the Clinton presidency, a pre-9/11 world, and budget surpluses. Cell phones were plastic dinosaurs too big to fit in our pocket. Email was in its infancy; Mark Zuckerberg was only ten years old. None of the *Friends* characters could text, tweet, swipe, snap, or Instagram their days away.

The main cast members of *Friends* are white, cisgender, heterosexual, middle-class, able-bodied, and good-looking. On the show, no one complains about being too "crazy busy" to meet up IRL (in real life). Instead, the *Friends* friends hang out *all the time*. Their dominant stage prop confirms this thesis: an overstuffed couch located in "Central Perk," the show's imaginary coffee house. The iconic piece of furniture now resides in Stage 48 of the Warner Brothers studio, and writer Adam Sternbergh says it symbolizes an era when we socialized face-to-face.

Today's biggest *Friends* fans never saw the show air in its original prime-time slot. Current college students, who might protest the homogeneity that they see in Hollywood, have fallen in love with its syndication. What *Friends* lacks in depth it makes up for in canned laughter, and younger Millennials and Generation Z (born mid-90s to mid-2000s) say it "reminds" them of the good ol' days they never knew.

Undergraduates are drawn to the show because of its now-impossible premise: Six young Americans take time to hang out (in person!) in a coffee shop—sans cell phones—and they *just* talk, building bonds that last a lifetime. No texts interrupt their conversation. No one is engrossed in documenting his or her life on Instagram. The friends just show up and spend time together. For young people, it's an absurd premise.

Friends also epitomizes the worry-free vibe that is both pre-9/11 and obscure to those teetering on adulthood. Millennials don't know what it's like to live in a world that doesn't include unsettling political, economic, and climate news. And with a twenty-four-hour news cycle, there's no escape from the stress.

Though the Internet connects us globally, it also interrupts the communities we have at home—like the premise of *Friends*. We now have less bandwidth for continuous, face-to-face time with loved ones. Trying to live like the *Friends* characters is a fantasy. We are wired and exhausted; our in-person social interactions (if we have them) are punctuated with taking selfies, checking Facebook, and Googling strange facts that arise in conversation. Prior to stumbling onto the new *Friends* obsession among my students, I thought I was the only one with nostalgia for the 1990s. It turns out there are sixteen million others like me who long for those days, but they didn't even live through them.

The 1990s weren't perfect, but they were less complicated when it came to sabbath. Weekends in small towns included resting, hanging out with friends, going to church, and forming community. There were still cliques and bullying, poverty and oppression. But there was also time spent *together*, doing nothing for the sake of nothing. Marta Kauffman, the cocreator of *Friends,* says she isn't surprised by the show's resurgence. Amid our modern connectivity, we are still lonely, craving close relationships like the ones we perceive between Chandler, Rachel, Monica, Joey, Ross, and Phoebe.[2]

The Conundrum

The sensible conclusion, then, is that we should all unplug and return to face-to-face interactions. But we don't because we can't get others to join us. When we tune out only to find everyone else is still tuned in, we feel even more alone.[3] Choosing to be a *Friends* friend in the tech era is a Sisyphean climb. I may put down my phone and plant myself on an overstuffed sofa in an urban coffee shop, but that doesn't mean anyone will join me. Besides, how would we coordinate our meet-up? Hardly anyone wants to chat on the phone anymore. If we can't text or message it, we often don't do it.

We are sabotaging ourselves from experiencing the "palace in time" that Rabbi Heschel describes. Because we "connect" via emojis, we fool ourselves into thinking that we're still cultivating meaningful bonds. But keeping in touch virtually (via text or email) doesn't provide the same psychological and communal benefits as in-person gatherings or long-distance phone calls. When I ask Fred if he thinks the pendulum will swing back the other way—whether we'll boycott our own cell phones and outlaw email—he doesn't think so. But I'm beginning to see the signs—literally. Waiting rooms now have placards with slashed cell phones, reminiscent of the no-smoking warnings of yore.

Some Americans are purposefully seeking out tech-free spaces such as retreat centers, spas, parks, hiking trails, and campsites. Still, since our modern culture and economy demand that we check and respond to emails and social media posts almost immediately, stepping out against tech may seem next to impossible. So what's the use?

Is Sabbath a Good Use of Time?

In his book, *Sabbath as Resistance: Saying No to the Culture of Now,* Walter Brueggemann describes sabbath as both countercultural and counter-economical. Brueggemann reminds us of the Israelites' enslavement in an Egyptian culture obsessed with productivity. The God of the enslaved Hebrew people is "sabbath-keeping, sabbath-giving, sabbath-commanding," the God who stands in sharp contrast to commerce.[4]

Times haven't changed much, according to the Old Testament scholar. We, like the ancient Israelites, continue to be shackled—but this time to the gods of Western culture: money, greed, fame, possessions, and consumerism. The Bible encourages us to avoid those things that keep us from knowing our internal self, God, and others.[5] Sabbath challenges us to resist the ways that other people and things control our time.

Marla Campbell, a professor of intercultural studies, describes what prioritizing sabbath time looks like. Sabbath, she says, is like large stones in a glass jar. When the stones are placed in the container first, as a priority, then the smaller things of life, like grains of sand, will sift around them. But if the little stuff (the sand, for example) is dumped in first, it takes up all the space, and the stones never fit.[6]

Numbering Our Days Rightly

Mark Buchanan, author of *The Rest of God: Restoring Your Soul by Restoring Sabbath,* writes that we are driven, time-managed, get-it-done people. Unfortunately, most of us reach a breaking point in our busyness: We forget the very reason we began striving for something in the first place. Drivenness, Buchanan notes, erodes purposefulness.[7]

Buchanan quotes Psalm 90:12, cautioning us to number our days rightly—not through ambition but in wisdom. "Numbering our days rightly" in the *eternal* sense is hard; we are well-equipped to track and achieve in finite time but not so good at cultivating that which transcends time. We fill our lives with schedules but miss the awe and wonder of unplanned time and space. We divide our lives into fifteen-minute Google calendar increments.

"Too much rigidity stifles purpose," Buchanan adds.[8] If we do what the psalmist suggests, we would be wise to number our days by another method. We should worry less about squeezing the life out of an hour and instead pay attention to the wonder of that hour. Those who savor life are neither preoccupied or obsessed with strangling productivity out of it.

Buchanan cites Jesus as an example of someone who numbered his days rightly. In his three-year ministry, Jesus operates without a detailed itinerary. As he hops around from one interruption to the next, he offers the gospel of his presence. Jesus wanders, detours, gathers, heals, teaches, retreats, answers, and delays, all while telling perplexing parables.

Jesus and his entourage are homeless, illogical in the material sense, and unattached. None of the disciples keep a daily checklist or tally Jesus' encounters and healings. They don't submit quarterly reports on progress made toward goals. And yet Jesus' ministry is successful, working toward a goal that makes no sense to the world: "Get to Jerusalem and die," as Buchanan states.[9]

Jesus lives a Spirit-led life, even in a culture trying to forbid him from performing acts of justice on the sabbath. He puts the over-planners on notice—the productive, wealthy, powerful, self-righteous, hoarders, ignorers, and worriers. He consistently calls us to the kind of action that isn't measured in qualitative data: love, justice, service, and awareness. Jesus even tells us that *he* comes to us in the form of an interruption: the "least of these" (Matt. 25:40). The hungry, the thirsty, the naked, and the imprisoned—all categories of people we tend to ignore in favor of getting things accomplished.

Buchanan reminds us that often the most meaningful moments of our lives are unplanned. It's what Buchanan calls the "crucible of interruptions"—the people, the relationships, and the moments that punctuate our days and remind us of our purpose—if only we will stop and pay attention. Our problem isn't a shortage of time but a shortage of noticing.[10]

Stop Day

Dr. Matthew Sleeth advocates for a "stop day" in his book *24-6: A Prescription for a Happier, Healthier Life.* He believes that Americans are overworked and overmedicated, frantic and rushing in a world in which we falsely believe one more piece of technology will give us more time and happiness. As hamsters on a wheel—working, surviving, providing—who has time for sabbath?

By not making time for rest, worship, and community each week, we may be losing up to eleven years of our lives.[11] As Americans, though, we hardly know what we're missing. We complain about being rushed, but we don't change our patterns to reclaim our lost decade. We balk at spending a full day at church, staying home to sit in solitude to pray, reading a book, or walking in nature without company or headphones. A month may go by, and we haven't shared a meal at home with our friends or called a loved one who lives across the country. We neglect to take a day to nap or play board games. Instead, our free time goes to huddling in front of a screen, reducing our human experience to 140 characters and filtered photos.

When we do manage to have a day "off," be it a Sunday or otherwise, we pack it with to-dos: errands, meals out, shopping, and entertainment. We can't or won't restrain ourselves from being plugged in and in motion, resulting in our relinquishment of opportunities for stopping, resting, worshiping, and connecting.

According to Sleeth, the fourth commandment is the biggest piece of the pie—the longest and most inclusive commandment of the ten given at Mount Sinai. Sleeth calls it the "fulcrum" because it bridges the first three, which deal with how we interact with God, with the last six, which deal with how we interact with one another.[12] Why, then, have we tossed out something so seemingly integral to our faith and lives?

Nearly three decades after the Fair Labor Standards Act, at the 1964 World's Fair in New York, sociologists warned Americans about the future problem of having too much leisure time on their hands, echoing the historic Puritan proverbial worry that "idle hands are the devil's workshop." Over fifty years later, it seems that we took this frightening possibility too seriously—and squeezed out any room for unmanaged hours.

According to Sleeth, work is up 15 percent in the last twenty years, and leisure time is down 30 percent.[13] But other researchers disagree; some say Americans actually work *less* than they did in the 1960s. What has shifted, Judith Shulevitz suggests, is Americans' *perception* of being pressed for time. More family members work outside the home, which means domestic tasks are divided among individuals. With the advent of email and texting, work projects spill into homelife.

Two-thirds of Americans work non-shift hours, meaning that they take work home, answering business emails, making calls, and texting their employees and colleagues during personal time. This disrupts our natural biological rhythms (circadian) and divides our attention constantly. As a result, we are never "off." Instead, we experience stress,

insomnia, inattentiveness, anxiety, depression, and overload.[14] Many of us
have become "work martyrs," a phrase coined by Project: Time Off, which
shows that 55 percent of Americans don't even use all their allotted vacation time in a year.[15] Studies also link greater occurrences of heart disease
to those who don't vacation.

Dan Buettner, author of *The Blue Zones: Eating and Living Like the
World's Healthiest People*, discovered a community of Seventh-day Adventists in Loma Lima, California, who take one entire day off per week for
sabbath. Combined with their vegetarian diet and access to health care,
they live an average of ten years longer than their American counterparts.
Buettner found that, like a weekly vacation, Seventh-day Adventists like
Aunt Glo attribute their longevity to keeping twenty-four hours of sabbath, allowing themselves to make time for God, for their relationships,
and for building a meaningful sense of community.[16]

Though science backs up the fact that humans need more boundaries between work and personal time, more vacation, more sleep, and less
screen time, we fear unplugging. And in some cases, we cannot afford
time off.

Sabbath as Economic Resistance

Today's culture often pressures us into believing that spending time with
our friends and family doesn't contribute to the bottom line. From an
early age, we learn Benjamin Franklin's adage from *Advice to a Young
Tradesman*: Time is money.

The 1938 Fair Labor Standards Act established parameters on the
forty-hour workweek that gave Americans weekend leisure time. In her
work on building the religious counterculture, Ana Levy-Lyons writes that
instead of using days off for rest, we use weekends to further boost the
economy. Shopping—rather than renewing ourselves through downtime,
spirituality, and time together—becomes the dominant weekend agenda.
Instead of relishing free time designed to release us from the mental and
physical load of work, we buy, do, and maintain—perhaps to escape our

fear of silence, stillness, and boredom. Weekends—or any time off in households—look like weekdays with regard to speed and productivity.[17]

The Puritans' warning of idle hands and leisure time seems to be ingrained in our DNA. Even when many Americans gained the weekend off, it became an excuse to remain busy, not slow down.

"I'll Sleep When I'm Dead."

Why don't we lean into the workweek established in the late 1930s? If we are privileged to have a day off, why don't we number our days rightly? Preacher and author Barbara Brown Taylor writes that sabbath time doesn't come naturally for Americans. Like Mark Buchanan, Taylor says that we are so caught up with our speed, our productivity, and our multi-tasking that setting aside one day to do nothing goal-oriented in the material sense can feel like death.[18] *Death*. Chasing our desires stems from our mortality—the pinch we feel in being finite. Our human limits lead us to embrace modern cultural and economic mottoes like YOLO (You Only Live Once) and FOMO (Fear of Missing Out).

So why do we equate slowing down with physical or economic death? Norman Wirzba, author of *Living the Sabbath: Discovering Rhythms of Rest and Delight*, suggests this feeling comes because we don't even stop enough to answer the question of why we are striving in the first place. What's it all for? Wirzba writes that sabbath is the weekly discipline to ask, ponder, and answer the questions that lead us into a more meaningful existence, not merely cogs in an economic or cultural wheel.[19]

Instead of using our days off for shopping or laundry, Wayne Muller writes that our time spent observing sabbath should be different from regular time. When we set aside this different kind of time—in spite of our fears of losing money, missing out, or, ultimately, death—we commit to remembering why we exist. Muller equates remembering the sabbath to a forest path that leads us back to ourselves. When we are fearful, overwhelmed, overburdened, and lost in the chaos, we only have to follow the path back inward. But the internal forest path is not our natural habitat.[20]

Wirzba suggests that to be countercultural is to evoke change. He makes a case not only for ceasing on the sabbath but also for patterning an entire lifestyle after the divine delight found in *menuchah*. Sabbath, then, becomes not a break from life but a source of life.[21]

The Struggle is Real

Ana Levy-Lyons thinks that we don't use days off to step out of the rat race because we have a deep-seated terror of unbridled free time.[22] Instead, we feel the need to plan to be in constant motion, even when not on the clock. We're "doing" something all the time, whether it's work-related, caregiving-related, household-related, screen-related, or simply running around from point A to B. Then, we wonder why we're so "crazy-busy" even on the weekends.

When free time yields to sabbath—unplanned sacred time for rest, worship, or gathered community—our worlds are turned upside down, and we feel uncomfortable. Sabbath practices are not what our culture or economy teaches us to do with our time. Observing sabbath is scary because it means slowing down to examine what we're doing with our lives, why we're doing it, and who we are. Sabbath, when practiced regularly, makes us realize what we've called "living" isn't actually living at all. The 24/7 age of frenzy doesn't mean anything in the grand scheme of things, especially in the face of death and limited time. That's a scary thought, so we avoid thinking about it.

Sabbath = Un-American?

The prospect of silence, solitude, or doing nothing goal-oriented in favor of spiritual pursuits not only feels frightening but also un-American. Our economic engine is fueled by faith that our daily work and consumer practices must go on—no matter what. Wartime economies are built on this premise. Sabbath practices of ceasing our labors, shopping, and to-dos disrupt the dominant logic of American culture. To partake in sabbath is to risk being seen as a navel-gazing, lazy, unproductive person. Though

Americans pride themselves on individualism, we follow the herd mentality when it comes to hard work and the American Dream.

If we are not advancing ourselves in the material sense each day, are we really American? We wear our busyness like a badge of honor, fearing the idea of taking time off, as it would disrupt the machine. Eventually, a mental, physical, or familial crisis hits, and Ana Levy-Lyons says it's then that we are forced to answer the ultimate question: Do we answer to God or to the world?[23]

But the very economic grit that Americans are so good at espousing could easily be transferred to spirituality. We must make time to seek answers to the questions that religion and spirituality ask us to consider: Where did I come from? Why am I here? How should I live? What is my purpose? There is a way forward, writes Dr. Monica Reed, author of "Beyond Sleep: Resting the Rest of You." The world was created with "divine blueprint," a balance of day and night, sun and moon. Sabbath naturally provides hours to consider these inquiries in our search for meaning. We aren't doing ourselves any favors by ignoring the One who created its rhythms.[24]

Sabbath Privilege

My postman wears a dark blue cowboy hat, reminiscent of what I believe must have been the United States Postal Service's dress code during the frontier days. We always exchange pleasantries. He only wants to chat for a minute, as he's busy sorting and shuffling envelopes and packages into my apartment complex's metal mail hub. He comments on the rain or the sunshine. Depending upon the day of the week, we'll talk about how great it is that it's Friday or how many days until Friday. Once, I asked him if he would be working on Saturday.

"I work six days a week, baby. Just Sundays off."

"But shouldn't you get another day off?" I asked, wondering why federal employees don't receive the standard two days I've learned about in my labor research.

"Nope. Just Sunday," he responded.

"Really?"

"And then I work three days at the hospital."

"Good grief," I said, feeling guilty for wrapping up my college teaching gig at 3:30 p.m. on a Friday.

"Duty calls, baby. Bills keep coming."

The postman tells me he'll only have to work his second job another year, which makes me wonder if he's trying to pay off a large bill—maybe sending kids to college—or trying to provide for family members.

My entire working career, with some exceptions, I've managed to avoid working weekends. This is both a privilege and responsibility, as I'm an individual who benefitted from garnering a specific set of skills that allows me to create a workweek-oriented schedule. But most Americans have at least two places they have to be, seven days a week. Retail and service-industries demand longer hours year after year to accommodate our weekend eating, shopping, and consuming.

Same-Day Delivery

I once ordered lavender oil and wool dryer balls from Amazon at 11:00 a.m. on a Saturday. At checkout, Amazon Prime notified me that my package would arrive the *same day*. I was suspicious.

"We'll see," I said to Fred.

Behind my cynicism was guilt. I didn't really need these eco-friendly dryer balls within eight hours. I'd already lived thirty-five years without them. I grew anxious when I thought about the logistical nightmare of getting them to my apartment by the afternoon. I imagined my purchase setting off a ping in a warehouse where a person, working on a Saturday, had to retrieve lavender oil and dryer balls from stacks numbered 3,588 and 72,539, on opposite sides of a million-square-foot building.

I thought about the worker climbing a dangerous ladder, cursing the fact that my order had to be retrieved from the top shelf. I heard his bitterness as he asked himself, *Why does she have to be so demanding? Who needs same-day delivery?* And then, I imagined an equally grumpy delivery person, irritated at making one trip out to an obscure address just so some eccentric lady could fancy herself "greener" for replacing her dryer sheets. "What privilege!" I thought I heard the delivery driver shout.

Truthfully, I have no idea how Amazon works. I know nothing about warehouse operations or delivery logistics. But I do know that the packages *did* arrive that night, and the guilt nearly crushed me. But I felt less terrible when I pulled warm, lavender-infused towels from the dryer. I am an American consumer after all.

Quicksand

One Friday night, I heard a holy man give a talk on American culture. He was visiting from far away, and his lecture attracted a crowd. As a monk, he spoke with an outsider's perspective few in the audience could fathom. He likened our addiction to productivity to quicksand—the more we move, the more we sink.

Contrary to intuition, one can escape quicksand by staying *still*. After some research, I learned that a friend shouldn't throw you rope to save you. The force needed to pull someone out of sinking sand is equivalent to that of hauling a medium-sized car. Instead, the trick is to lean back, allowing the density of the human body to float to the top of the quicksand. Then, the victim can free his or her legs and slowly get out. Frenzy and fighting don't help. Only when we are motionless, leaning back and looking up, can we be saved. God, who transcends culture and economics, holds the key to escaping our proverbial quicksand. When we look heavenward, we discover the extent to which we exist as spiritual beings. With legs and feet free, we find ourselves on solid ground, feeling steadier than we did mired in the quicksand of ego, achievement, and success.

45-Percent Life Crisis

I love birthdays. I'm that enthusiastic person who insists that people should take a week—no, make that a month—to celebrate their birthday. I mark loved ones' big days on my calendar with great anticipation, and I look forward to celebrating their lives. Typically, I meet my own birthday with the same vigor. I see it as an opportunity to reflect upon the year: What have I accomplished? What goals have I met? Where have I traveled? What have I read? What lessons have I learned?

Last year was different. I met my thirty-fifth birthday with dread. The US life expectancy is around seventy-eight years, and I was nearly 45 percent done with this mortal coil. I was angry with God for my chronic migraine diagnosis and my declining health, cursing the time passing under my nose. I had only 55 percent battery life remaining. Loved ones were dying, and my mother's cognition was fading, which meant that the earliest pieces of my identity were fading too. I had arrived at the existential crisis we all have when we're not too busy to notice it: We're dying. We're losing our connections. Typically, we're too swamped with to-do lists to have a meltdown about how short and temporary life is.

The "Dopomax" side effects ceased just after my thirty-fifth birthday. I resented that they had made me feel like I was walking through Jell-O, but they also brought me clarity: I was depressed. I had neither zest nor motivation for the events that usually brought me joy (like birthdays). I took a step back to reassess what it all meant. It served as a wake-up call to find better medical treatment (ultimately Botox) and to revisit sabbath. I needed to return to what I'd been taught in the sleepy towns of Dana, Indiana, and Reidsville, North Carolina. My birthday came with an invitation to seek self-care outside the pressures of culture and economy. It also offered the gift of noticing—noticing my own mortality and my need to opt out of being "on" all the time. I was being invited to a space of wrestling with deeper questions. I could easily accept the invitation to meet myself, God, and others again. I only had to look up, lean back, and have faith; only then would I float to the top of the quicksand.

4

A DIFFERENT CALLING

You were called to freedom, brothers and sisters; only don't let
this freedom be an opportunity to indulge your selfish impulses,
but serve each other through love.

—GALATIANS 5:13-14, CEB

About the time I began the chronic migraine clinical study, Fred and I started gathering with friends two Friday nights per month to study scripture, pray, and eat. Fred and I didn't launch this initiative; three families with three children *each*—who are far busier than we are—created the group. The evenings are friendly and informal. One young monk who lives in western North Carolina drives four hours to teach our lesson. His wisdom is punctuated by restless children and eager questions. After our study, no one is in a rush to return home. No clocks adorn the walls around us; we eat slowly and catch up on one another's lives, often bemoaning the hectic pace we feel outside our Friday nights. We sense freedom in our kvetching, as the workweek slog is still two days away. On these Friday nights, we recline in the balm of sabbath.

This group of people hails from a religious tradition that has no theology of sabbath. It's neither Jewish nor Christian; no seven-day Creation story can be found in its holy scriptures. Rather, it's my Hindu husband's *sanga*, a faith community within his religion. I'm an outsider, but they welcome me with open arms, though I view their scripture through a christological lens. The Hindu religion doesn't command a sabbath practice, but this small group has chosen to implement one. Our busiest Hindu friends—those with kids and jobs and houses—sought out this space and time, and the rhythm of six-and-one is not even a part of their sacred narrative.

Our Friday night gathering was birthed from families committed to exploring and teaching their children about *real* life—that is, the *spiritual* life. Any faith group—Baptists, Methodists, Catholics, Buddhists—could start a sabbath Friday night (or Tuesday night or any night) ritual like this one. They only need to lean into what people of faith are called to do: step out of the ordinary and into the sacred.

They'll Know We Are Christians by Our Sabbath

A few years ago, a friend introduced me to Kate Rademacher, a Christian convert (from Unitarian Universalism) who is married to a Buddhist.[1] Kate and I bonded first over interfaith marriage, and when we had lunch, she asked a myriad of questions about *Saffron Cross*, a book that chronicles my marriage to a devout Hindu. The sabbath-keeping chapter particularly stood out to her.

"In the book, why did you equate sabbath-keeping with only worship?" she asked. Her question stumped me.

My Baptist roots taught me that sabbath was synonymous with church-going. Like my mother and Aunt Gail, I'd learned that Sunday church attendance was non-negotiable. Both sides of my family showed me that we kept sabbath by worshiping in community and praising God through hymns and long, Bible-based sermons. Sunday always meant church, and we began the day with alleluia (or Saraluia!) and ended it the same way. Kate's question encouraged me to consider what other dimensions of sabbath I had missed. What was sabbath beyond the anchor of liturgy? Does the Lord's Day require more of us than sitting in pews?

Although I always had equated sabbath with worship, Kate posed her question at a time when I had been playing church-hooky a lot. As a teen, I wouldn't have dreamt of missing a service. But my love affair with Sunday worship had become an obligation. The shine had worn off.

Later, I learned that Kate's inquiry stemmed from her own sabbath struggles as a newly baptized Christian. She'd grown up in the Unitarian Universalist (UU) tradition in one of the most liberal communities in Massachusetts. Her intellectual parents had chosen a faith for her that gave her a foundation of community impact; she learned early that making a difference in the lives of others was essential to spirituality.

Kate told me that Unitarian Universalism both blessed and frustrated her. In the UU church, Kate learned about a broad spectrum of the world's religions, but she was left to determine what traditions, beliefs, and spiritual disciplines worked for her. This cafeteria-style buffet of faith choices led her to want to go deeper. As a response to this yearning, Kate's UU minister encouraged her to join a nine-month workshop to explore various approaches to spirituality. Through that seminar, Kate was first drawn to the concept of sabbath as well as to an initial discovery of God through the incarnation of Jesus. These a-ha moments of sabbath and Christ directed her to the Episcopal tradition (a denomination of her ancestors), where she converted and was baptized in her thirties.[2]

As an earnest convert, Kate was energized by the discipline of a faith and praxis with parameters, as opposed to a generalist approach that overwhelmed her. While she was filled to the brim with gratitude for her new Christian community, she still felt lonely in her quest for a Christian sabbath practice. Kate named the discrepancy. Her faith community would recite the Decalogue (Ten Commandments) during services, but after a brief fellowship time, many would exit the church quickly. Some parishioners told her they needed to go grocery shopping or answer work emails. No matter what duty called, it was offered in a tone that made it seem like Sunday afternoon was *ordinary*—not *sacred*—time.

Kate admits she naïvely thought that all Christians practiced a strict sabbath wherein Sunday wasn't anything like every other day. From her theological and scripture studies leading up to her baptism, she envisioned sabbath as an *entire day* of rest, devotion, worship, and community—a day both blissful and expansive. Jesus and sabbath were the very elements that drew her to the Christian faith. When she joined the church, she imagined the community would help keep her accountable to Jesus' teachings and observing God's gift of sabbath.

The worship hour was meaningful—but she found that her fellow Christians spent the remainder of Sunday checking off their to-do lists. Rather than leaning into the invitation to twenty-four hours of deepening her faith, Kate's Christian sabbath felt compartmentalized. Though her church community offered her the discipline of a single, deep path she'd yearned for, she still felt that something was missing. Kate wondered when, how, and why Christians had stopped observing the entire day for sabbath. Why would they choose to miss out on God's gift of rest for creation? In keeping with Rabbi Bach's explanation of the seven-day Creation narrative and the Hebrew term *menuchah*, Kate resonated with the idea that the world is not complete without God-ordained sacred rest—the kind we should seek throughout the entire sabbath day and not merely an hour on Sunday morning.

Like many career-oriented thirty-somethings, Kate believes in the calling she strives for during the other six days of the week. Her work is important to her. She's been programmed to be productive, impactful, and efficient, part of God's mandate to do good in the world. But she also believes that she's called to rest. Her priests continued to reinforce this message, but Kate felt lonely in her sabbath praxis.

Sabbath Buddies

Kate voiced her concerns at a church small-group gathering and asked if anyone else felt a need to make sabbath more intentional and accountable. A seventy-five-year-old retiree said that she too longed for more sabbath. Together they became "sabbath buddies."

Kate and her sabbath buddy committed to monthly check-ins before and after Sunday, and Kate started to feel less alone. But she also didn't feel it was the same as *the entire* community of believers being accountable to one another. The sabbath buddy system didn't have the weight of the congregation on its side. Their check-ins were not deemed an official, sacramental practice—certainly not one mandated from the pulpit like baptism or Communion—or even found under the umbrella of a Lenten observance. But like Rabbi Bach explained, Kate understood her priests' desire to meet people where they are, which includes being empathetic to those who cannot strictly observe the fourth commandment because of personal or familial circumstances. The very sabbath intention, expectation, and discipline Kate longed for may be unattainable to her pewmate.

Today's pastors lead attendance-declining Christian communities in an instant gratification society not conducive to being formed and guided about how they spend their time. Priests also shepherd members from all socioeconomic backgrounds and circumstances, some of whom are obligated to work on Sundays. To deem Sundays as strictly sabbath could leave a portion of the congregants feeling isolated and unsupported. Still, Kate wondered why, with Christ as the head of the church, Christian parishes weren't at least trying to be more countercultural and counter-economic when it came to sabbath. But because churchgoers are already overcommitted and feel the pinch of what they perceive as less free time, pulpit mandates about not shopping on Sundays could lead to an even sharper decline in American Christianity, which, according to the Pew Research Center's America's Changing Religious Landscape data, has dropped a percentage point per year in the last seven years (down from 78.4 percent in 2007 to 70.6 percent in 2014).[3]

While Kate's clergy advocate for sabbath, they are cognizant of the mounting pressures parishioners face when it comes to time: work, parenting, caregiving, domestic upkeep, and survival. Most parish staff are just happy to see congregants cross the sanctuary threshold for an hour on Sundays. With this in mind, most ministers choose to encourage those in the pews rather than chastise them with strict sabbath parameters.

Kate wonders how the church could be countercultural while also taking its cues from American culture. How might sabbath benefit from an upgrade: better packaging, making it more *marketable* and *sellable*—two terms that would probably make Jesus want to flip some tables. The church, amid its call to be different, could leverage sabbath as an unopened gift, drawing new converts and weary old-timers seeking devotion and connection. For Kate and others like her, sabbath as spiritual and communal self-care might be just the retooling the fourth commandment needs.

Mothers, Be Good to Your Daughters

The modern woman's experience is complex. Many adult women were raised by first- and second-wave feminist mothers and grandmothers, matriarchs who lived through the Women's Movement and were the first to work outside the home.

Young girls are now groomed to believe they can be both strong and tender, striking a balance between career warriors and effective caregivers. Today's woman can do and be anything: a CEO, a surgeon, a firefighter, a chef—all while telling bedtime stories and caregiving for those around her. Women now balance a strong drive to succeed with a heart for nurturing. Unfortunately, these ideas also create societal and cultural expectations that can reinforce the stress of always "on" and can lead to anxiety.

Kate remembers her own rearing by an educated mother and community that instilled in her a strong work ethic and ambition. By her high-school years, Kate felt pressured to be effective. She went on to study at Wesleyan University, one of the most esteemed liberal arts colleges in the country, but daily panic attacks controlled her life. She longed for a different way of living. After college graduation, she sought balance by leaving the competitive Northeast, eventually moving to North Carolina to live and serve in a rural farm and intentional community.

Kate's experience is not unique; many women struggle with the pressure of having careers, raising children, and managing their families' daily routines—which doesn't include time for spiritual growth. Kate, who works for a global nonprofit organization that focuses on international public health, recalled a recent conversation with a female coworker.

After an exhausting week, the two of them leaned against a wall, bemoaning how challenging it was to be full-time moms while having full-time, successful careers.

"Maybe our daughters will it figure out," Kate's coworker said.

"No!" Kate balked, "I want to figure it out *for* my daughter."

Like my mother and Aunt Gail, who replayed Grandmother Evelyn's sabbath rules back to her and to Aunt Frances at the most inopportune time, today's women are showing the next generation how to do it all. Kate wants to teach her daughter that God doesn't intend for her to live a frazzled and harried life. She hopes to instill in her that we are called both to work and to sabbath.

It all comes back to intention and accountability. How do we teach children to prioritize their spiritual lives when we can't model it? How will they know the importance of rest, worship, and community when congregations don't talk about sabbath? How does the church show its youngest members the value of rest when grown-ups can't even hold themselves accountable to a sabbath standard?

A Child Shall Lead Them

Sabbath mirrors a child's world. Most kids don't have a sense of urgency. I've noticed this whenever I see a friend with kids ask them to put on their shoes and get ready to leave the house. An hour later, they *might* be in the car. Children have no need for efficiency; instead, they are full of joy and wonder. They dillydally and stop to ask a million questions. Children live in the moment; they experience the world at their own pace and usually without an end goal in mind. They create worlds completely in their own imagination, make-believing until sundown. In the age of what Kate calls "distracted parenting," adults should take cues from their tiny counterparts. Kate's weekly sabbath intention includes spending time with her daughter in non-goal-oriented play.

During sabbath, Kate always accepts an invitation from her daughter to smash rocks in the driveway or to draw a treasure map of their neighborhood. The rocks are not contributing to a landscaping project; the map is not to scale. What's being "accomplished" during these hours of play is all for fun. Kate's daughter simply wants to be together and explore ideas—ones that may seem frivolous to the outside world.

One sabbath afternoon, Kate's daughter became upset and locked herself in the bathroom. Instead of demanding that she come out at once, Kate simply laid down outside the bathroom door and passed her daughter a handwritten note. They slid the paper back and forth, jotting down new messages to each other for twenty minutes.

During ordinary time, Kate might not have leaned into this kind of activity. But it was sabbath. She slowed down, let the Spirit in, and allowed her daughter to show her the way. Kate felt no rush to get her daughter out of the bathroom; she was present in the moment. When her daughter finally emerged, they returned to their game outside, giggling and connected.

Do Whatever You Want

After her conversion, Kate asked her priest how she should keep the sabbath. "What's better? Saturday or Sunday?" Kate's priest explained that either was okay and guided her to do what worked best for her and her family. The clergyperson knew Kate was a conscientious new Christian and that she'd give her all to whatever sabbath choice she made. This advice is similar to what most empathetic ministers would offer, careful not to add any additional stress to their flock's busy lives. They know congregants work several jobs and raise children. Society's modern complexity makes them trepidatious about offering specific instructions as a mandate to the entire community. One sabbath size doesn't necessarily fit all.

But Kate wishes her clergy would offer some stricter sabbath confines. This is where Kate finds herself drawn to the Jewish practice of sabbath, which has a set time for sabbath's beginning and end. Kate loves the idea that at Friday sundown, laundry is dropped mid-fold, errands are stopped, and computers are turned off. Candles are lit, prayers are said, services are attended, and dinners are shared. Time with God and community ensues on a timeline not of our own making (but of the Creator's), and ordinary tasks vanish for twenty-four hours. Could the body of Christ offer its members something similar? Since the Jews have perfected this art form, Christians could return to their Hebrew roots but view them through Christ.

Kate also wonders if ministers could use the very technology that tethers us to the world to help us regain our true lives. Might we rekindle a love for sabbath through a sermon series, newsletter blurbs, and email blasts? Still, the Christian church, unlike its Jewish brothers and sisters, faces a problem: Christians across all denominations don't have definitive lines for when sabbath begins and ends or instructions for how it should be observed. Among Protestants, only Seventh-day Adventists observe strict twenty-four-hour sabbath rules, keeping in line with Jesus' ancient Hebrew practice of Saturday. The Mormon Church observes sabbath on Sunday, while most Catholic parishes still hold mass on Saturday evenings. Contemporary nondenominational churches might even schedule a weeknight worship service. Christianity, unlike Judaism, has different ideas about when sabbath starts and ends and what constitutes its practices. Kate and other American workers like her fall into a category of employees whose work culture expects them to be "on" beginning Sunday. As the Monday workday blurs into Sunday afternoon or evening, this period of time becomes another space where unplugging is hard.

Rabbi Bach says that a teacher once told him a true day off is one in which you don't have to shave—literally or metaphorically. In other words, the sabbath expectation is that we shouldn't prepare ourselves for any work in the ordinary sense. Sabbath should encompass a space where societal and economic expectations and consequences cease. On Sunday afternoons, Kate feels like she has to "shave" in the metaphorical sense. As the evening approaches, she begins preparing for the slog of the workweek ahead, starting with emails. But everyone in Kate's office seems to respect the boundaries of Saturday. An unspoken rule among her work team says that no one checks email that day. Sunday afternoon, however, is fair game. What, then, are Christians to do? How are we to be faithful to God, sabbath, and the church?

Kate wonders if the Hebrew notion of sabbath (Friday night to Saturday night) might work better, given our societal structure. In most American workweeks, Friday night marks a delineation between work and fun,

Saturday continues along that vein (with the addition of household tasks), and Sunday becomes the bridge to work. Sunday morning church services, then, could cap off a sabbath observance, a time to leave God's world of sacred time and enter ordinary time. Based on what Kate has seen in her parish, this method might work, as few are able to keep sabbath *after* morning worship. Could the generous sabbath portion of Friday–Saturday with a bookend on Sunday at noon infuse the entire workweek with a sense of God's call and mission?

Kate wishes the church would tell her what to do. By establishing the strict lines (and rules) of sabbath, she feels like she'd have both the permission and the heft of the community behind her—no matter what day was chosen. For Jews, the sabbath has remained the seventh day (based on Sunday being the first day) because "it is written." Since Jewish communities around the world observe sabbath each week, it sticks. The Seventh-day Adventists are good at this too. They stand by their Jewish brothers and sisters' parameters of a twenty-four-hour Saturday sabbath, but they are the only modern Christians to consistently do so.

As a recent convert, it grieves Kate that she has no benchmark to start and end the holy day—no common practice across the great swath of Christianity. This can make new converts like Kate feel as if Christ's followers are not as committed to the commandment of sabbath as they ought to be. But Christianity is so diverse, it would be nearly impossible to agree on how to observe the fourth commandment worldwide. Christians can't even agree on how to baptize and share Communion.

While the danger of sabbath intentions and parameters might drive away people because they feel like obligations, not observing sabbath at all can leave us feeling self-centered. If we practice the Jewish or Christian faith, then sabbath orders our lives rightly; it makes God the Creator and us the blessed recipients of creation and rest. When we determine that we can do whatever we like on the sabbath (whatever day we observe it), we become a pick-and-choose culture, keeping what we want and getting rid of what's hard. This isn't what spirituality is about; practice is difficult because it helps us grow in faith. We cannot observe Easter without Good Friday.

"It's a rule," Kate reminded me, citing the Ten Commandments. Though I was born and bred in the church, even I forget that sabbath is a commandment. And when I was a child, these very rules—the boundaries and structure they create—kept me from danger, even as I learned and made mistakes. We should remind ourselves that God is our holy parent, and God's rules exist for a purpose—to keep us safe, happy, and healthy.

A Welcome Mat

Kate's friendship has given me a fresh perspective. I'd never thought about a convert's view of sabbath, someone for whom the gift of *menuchah* is new and rare. Yet this gift is often left on the shelf, gathering dust, by a tradition in need of its offerings.

Christians are good at outreach, hospitality, evangelism, programming, and coffee hours—but our growth edge is making room for and strengthening spiritual practices. Once folks find a home in our pews (whether as infants, teens, adults, or older adults), we do them a disservice by ignoring the praxis that keeps us all deeply rooted. Now is the time to reexamine sabbath. With the steady decline in church attendance, we should observe what's working well and where we've missed the mark.

I see an entire American culture yearning for sabbath. People are sending out emergency signals, begging for relief from their stressed-out, overworked, desperate lives. People want rest, devotional practices, and community. They want real life—the kind of meaning we only find amid the Divine. The God of Abraham has an ancient gift to offer, a spiritual technology that transcends every generations' distractions and woes. What would it take for the Christian church to embrace sabbath as a weekly launch into a deeper life? What would it mean to provide answers for converts like Kate, who have come to the faith seeking solutions but haven't yet found what they hoped for?

If the church wants to save sabbath, it must act quickly and decisively, offering refuge from the pressures of daily life and creating a community that looks different from the world outside its doors.

5

SABBATH AS REST

*"Come to me, all you that are weary and are carrying heavy burdens, and
I will give you rest. Take my yoke upon you, and learn from me; for I am
gentle and humble in heart, and you will find rest for your souls. For my
yoke is easy, and my burden is light."*
—MATTHEW 11:28-30

Our heart is restless until it rests in you.
—SAINT AUGUSTINE, *THE CONFESSIONS, CHAPTER 1*

My chronic migraine diagnosis had led me down the path I needed to
travel. The Botox injections were working; the "Dopomax" effects had
cleared. Rabbi Bach steered me toward the gift of Judaism's "spiritual
technology." Kate reminded me of Christianity's calling to live *differently,*
including the practice of sabbath. The spiritual medicine was helping. I
was gaining the tools I needed to dive back into a sabbath reminiscent of
my childhood. The framework of sabbath practice—rest, worship, and
community—awaited me.

Rest, Actually

In the mid-1980s, Holiday Company opened a franchise hotel chain called Embassy Suites. The first time I walked through the doors of the one in Indianapolis, I just knew Manhattan had relocated herself. I wasn't even a decade old, but I was certain that the Big Apple had arrived in flyover country. Every subsequent Embassy Suites I've stayed in gives me the same feeling. It's not a Ritz-Carlton (not that I've seen one of those), but it's American middle-class pampering at its best—I can *smell* the luxury wafting from the free breakfast buffet.

Each afternoon, the Embassy Suites hosts a happy hour with free drinks and finger foods; one time, I even met an aging hippie giving complimentary massages on a folding black seat. Strategically placed jungle plants make guests believe they've escaped to a luxurious spa in Costa Rica, though the Dollar General is one mile away. In my opinion, no other hotel chain pulls off both elegance and accessibility as well as they do.

The draw of the Embassy Suites—or any decent hotel—is the invitation to rest. I am one of those persons who hasn't evolved past the requisite eight hours of sleep per night—or else. Ten hours is ideal, really. Fewer than eight leaves me short-fused. Fred and I fight the most when I'm sleep-deprived. He'll say something innocuous, and my temper flares. I summon my Oscar-worthy performance for Best Actress in a Motion Picture, stomping out of our apartment with purse in hand, declaring, "I'm going to the Embassy Suites!" Then I'll drive to the grocery store and sit in the parking lot for a respectable amount of time before returning home. By then, Fred has sent a sweet text.

Bouts of terrible insomnia notwithstanding, this exchange happens a few times per year. I always threaten to leave for my favorite hotel chain, but I never get there. But the Embassy Suites has become a symbol in our household: a bastion of retreat when I've had enough. It's a metaphor for the kind of radical rest only achievable in a clean king-size bed and a generically decorated room. It's that empty physical and mental space that comes with high thread counts and blackout curtains.

The more our lives speed up, the more we need our own version of the Embassy Suites. Tangible respite works—whether a towering hotel, a long nap, or an uninterrupted night's sleep. These oases are few and far between—especially when we find ourselves short on cash, serving as the primary caregiver for children and loved ones, or working multiple jobs. Even when we have the needed resources, we often don't think to use them for *rest*.

The Sleep Revolution

In April 2016, media mogul Arianna Huffington published *The Sleep Revolution: Transforming Your Life, One Night at a Time.* A hit with always-tired Americans, the book rose to the top of *The New York Times* Best Sellers list. Every celebrity Instagram feed featured the tome and perfectly coiffed famous people posing in navy sleep masks. Huffington's work asserts that better sleep is the antidote to everything. She writes that sleep deprivation undermines our relationships, our purpose, and our lives. Huffington also shines light on our Western culture's dismissal of sleep as something for the weak and unmotivated.

But studies refute the conclusion that we are getting less sleep. According to the Bureau of Labor Statistic's Annual American Time Use Survey, the average civilian slept 8.83 hours per day in 2015.[1] So why do we *feel* so sleep deprived? Much debate surrounds this question. Are we lacking quality sleep? Are we expecting too much by insisting on eight consecutive hours (we know that our predecessors did a lot of "segmented sleep"). Or is it that we can't turn off our brains at night? Is the pre-bedtime screen time (smartphones, TVs, or other devices) the culprit? The answer is likely yes, yes, and yes. When we check email before bed or send a quick text, our "on" time bleeds into our "off" time. Or we may stay off our handheld devices but binge watch our guilty pleasure or the twenty-four-hour news cycle before bed. No matter what, this mental stimulation keeps us from winding down. At the end of the day, when our brains are ready to decompress, we give them more data to process. And when we have more to process, we have more to be anxious about. Because our screens stay out until we fall asleep (and some of us even sleep holding them), we have no firm boundary between the waking and sleeping hours.

Resting Our Eyes

In the midafternoon, when my grandparents were tired, they used to say, "I just need to rest my eyes for a minute." They would not necessarily go to bed for a two-hour nap, but they would sit in a chair or lie on the couch, close their eyes, and be silent for a while. Swiftly and soundly, they tuned out the world with the ease of a seasoned meditation practitioner. Besides my favorite septuagenarians, I can't remember the last time I saw anyone *rest* in a chair or *sleep* on the sofa—without reaching for his or her phone.

Americans have an awful time resting.

Stimuli surround us: TVs, phones, tablets, and computers. Visit any public or private place and something will be beeping or blasting, begging for attention. Waiting rooms, checkout lines, carpool lanes, commutes, and lunch breaks are filled with people staring at phones, unwilling to allow themselves time simply to stare off into space for a minute or to close their eyes and rest.

Don't Just Do Something, Sit There

We know we need more quality sleep—or time to "rest our eyes"—but we are addicted to our phones, children cry in the middle of the night, insomnia hasn't been eradicated, and most workplaces do not yet offer nap pods. So what do we do?

In "Beyond Sleep: Resting the Rest of You," Dr. Monica Reed writes that *solitude* can actually offer some of the deepest, most fulfilling and rejuvenating forms of rest. When our check engine lights are on, as Reed describes it, lighting up from stress, irritability, anxiety, indecision, or exaggeration of a minor problem, alone time can help us recalibrate.[2] But we fight system maintenance. Perhaps we fear solitude—because we don't want to be alone with our thoughts.

A 2014 University of Virginia study confirms this. Participants were asked to sit quietly by themselves in a room with nothing to do but think. Prior to entering the space, participants were shown a button that, when pressed, delivers a shock. When asked if they would ever willingly press the button, most said they would pay *not to be shocked.*

Finding themselves in a room alone with nothing to do but "think, ponder, or daydream," participants found that it "wasn't very enjoyable" and it was "hard to concentrate." Some cheated and admitted to getting out of their seat and checking a phone. Others even *willingly* administered the electronic shock they said they'd pay to forgo.[3] And here's the most interesting part: Results were similar across age demographics. These days, apparently, *no one* can "rest their eyes."

All by Myself

From an early age, we're told that humans are *communal* creatures. We are meant to be *together,* from the Creation story of Adam and Eve to Noah and the flood, we survive and thrive with a plus-one. Being alone is dangerous, we're warned. We're taught to use the buddy system and told not to walk alone at night. Too much alone time leads to isolation or depression and substance abuse, we're told.

While we think of fear of solitude as a modern anxiety, it's not. In *Pensées,* mathematician and philosopher Blaise Pascal postulates that all of humanity's problems stem from our inability to sit in a room alone. Pascal was writing in the 1600s—what would he think of the UVA study?

But there have always been humans who value solitude and thrive on it. Ancient and modern mystics and monastics, the early church's desert mothers and fathers, and general recluses have mastered the art of being alone. The great faith teachers whose wisdom remains today—Jesus, the Buddha, Gandhi, Saint Teresa of Calcutta—modeled solitude and silence. Why is it so hard for us?

A Silent DJ

Vanna Fox is a clergywoman and dear friend who used to talk for a living. She is a North Carolina celebrity, her distinct Southern drawl and velvet voice standing out amid the pack of Raleigh radio announcers and DJs.

I first met Vanna completely out of context, while attending the Wild Goose Festival, a transformational, experiential festival grounded in faith-inspired social justice, for which she now serves as senior vice president. I didn't recognize her face; I only recognized her voice.

Vanna is energetic, gregarious, and talkative (in the best sense of the word). That's why I was surprised to learn that for the past ten years, she has kept a monthly sabbath practice of at least twenty-four hours of *silence, solitude,* and fasting. It's not that I couldn't imagine Vanna sitting quietly by herself, but silence and solitude are unusual practices for anyone in the modern world, especially for a woman who made a career out of talking to half a million listeners each week. But Vanna insists that being silent and solitary is how she came to simply listen for God.

In Vanna's monthly practice, her silence and solitude help her remember and pray for others. She says that restricting her voice clears her mind and spirit. In turn, this sabbath practice spills over into her daily life. It helps her walk with others without judgment. She can care for and listen without fixing or projecting an outcome. Beside monastics, Vanna is the only person I have ever met who regularly keeps an extended amount of quiet time by herself.

Martha, Martha

When I was first tried to lean into the sabbath rhythm of rest, I felt guilty and suspicious, confronted with the internal urge to achieve. *Is resting really a good investment of time? Shouldn't I be doing something more productive?*

No, the Spirit said. *Sit. Rest. Just be.*

My predicament reminds me of how Jesus redirects Martha in Luke 10. After Martha complains that her sister, Mary, isn't helping her prepare Jesus' meal, he responds: "Martha, Martha, you are worried and distracted by many things; there is need of only one thing. Mary has chosen the better part, which will not be taken away from her" (vv. 41-42).

Martha, Martha, I tell myself, shaking my head. Sometimes I *still* don't get the message.

Sabbath, the Spirit reminds me. *Menuchah. There is no better to-do list.*

The Best Laid Plans

In *Keeping the Sabbath Wholly: Ceasing, Resting, Embracing, Feasting*, Marva J. Dawn writes that church, unfortunately, is not where we go to find rest, solitude, or silence. Church can often be everything *but* renewing. Often, we leave our faith communities with more to-dos than when we arrived, which is why church, in the modern era, is not synonymous with *menuchah*. Rest, solitude, and silence, then, remain in the commercial and private realm.

We might pamper ourselves with a day at the spa or a night at the Embassy Suites. This kind of rest isn't necessarily bad, but it's still tied to capitalism—producing and consuming. It lacks a key component of restorative, sabbath rest: alone time, in silence, to do nothing related or pertaining to the world.

Last summer, amid the swirl of migraines and recovery, I was desperate for rest—but not the kind I could find at the Embassy Suites. I wanted *spiritual* rest—time like Vanna's—for solitude, silence, and sleep in a Christian retreat setting. Fellow Duke Divinity School friends had visited Trappist monasteries; others had enrolled in two-year spiritual formation programs where they retreated every quarter. Some made pilgrimages to the Holy Land. A restful, solitary, and silent spiritual retreat had appealed to me for years. I wanted something bold—but close to home—a catalyst that would launch me into a new sabbath-as-rest routine that was too difficult to establish surrounded by my daily responsibilities and worries.

Sabbath Retreat, Act I: The Perfect Storm

I chose a Catholic retreat center about forty minutes from my apartment. It was quasi-familiar; years ago, I'd co-led a retreat there for the women of my church. This time, though, I would not be responsible for programming anyone but myself.

I arrived on a Wednesday morning in June, a half hour late as is my custom. The morning rush hour had made me anxious and frenzied, and I was already worried about managing my sabbath time to a tee. I'd calculated that this retreat was going to cost me $4 per hour, so I needed to make the best use of my time—even when I was asleep.

The deacon on duty welcomed me. He told me I would be the only retreatant there for the next two days, so my request for spiritual rest via silence and solitude could be accommodated easily. I welcomed this news, checking off boxes in my head and feeling as if I had already achieved something. He ushered me to a building that contained a hallway of small, monastic cells like the one I imagined anchorites like Julian of Norwich occupied. There were five rooms on the hall and two bathrooms. My ten by ten chamber contained only a small desk, chair, twin bed, lamp, and alarm clock. I had to maneuver carefully around the end of the bed just to unpack. The room had two doors: one to the hall and one to the backyard, where a slim concrete sidewalk ran along the back of the building. A rocking chair sat on the sidewalk under the eaves.

It was a clear day, the hottest part of which had not yet arrived. I was drawn outside to explore. Guilt followed. *Why are you wasting time walking around? You need to dig into your spiritual work,* I thought. *The clock is ticking. Four dollars per hour, Dana. Get it done.* Only fifteen minutes in, and I had already applied the wrong set of "rules" to sabbath rest, thinking I was going to get the "work" of renewal, solitude, and silence accomplished.

I fought the need to quantify sabbath and explored my surroundings instead. I paused in front of a Saint Francis statue. Francis always looks content, bird in hand and rabbit at his feet. I got my phone out to snap his picture. *This will make an awesome Twitter post,* I thought.

Caught again.

Dana, can you please stop? You're here to rest by yourself and silence the noise of the world. Put the phone away.

I was distracted, thankfully, by a stone labyrinth down the hill from where I stood. Usually, I'm too impatient to actually *walk* a labyrinth. Instead, I typically head straight to its center, defeating the entire purpose of the practice. It's a metaphor for my life: I love the achievement but hate the process. I'd read about this particular labyrinth in the welcome pamphlet the deacon had given me. Like sabbath, the labyrinth is a path, not a result. Its design is much like the sabbath blueprint. We begin at the outside of the circle, which signifies our lives in the world. As we weave through the path toward the center—a process called *shedding*—we leave behind ordinary time and tasks. When we arrive at the center, we receive *illumination*, or a higher understanding. The center of any labyrinth typically has a place to stand, sit, leave something behind, receive something, and feel the presence of the Divine.

Winding our way out of the labyrinth is a metaphor for returning to the world, only equipped with some mystical learning from the center. The labyrinth, then, mirrors sabbath: we rest, we turn inward, we turn toward God, and then we return to the world—but this time more connected. Somehow, the same path that leads us to the center also leads us back into the world as changed people.

I stood at the opening of this labyrinth, determined to walk the entire thing. An inscribed paver greeted me: "Write your hurts in the sand. Carve your blessings in stone." I walked mindfully along the rock-lined, mulched circle, coming upon strategically placed markers just when I was about to lose my intention and attention. "This is holy ground," one read.

When I finally made my way to the center (it was the first time I'd walked an entire labyrinth without going directly to the middle), I sat down on the bench, feeling accomplished. Beneath my feet were the words, "Make me an instrument," the beginning of the prayer famously attributed to Saint Francis. I sat for a while, kicking at pebbles, contemplating how sabbath makes us instruments of peace to sow seeds of love, pardon, faith, hope, light, and joy. After a time, I exited the center and worked my way back around the circumference, where I met another marker: "New dawn, new day, new life."

In exploring this new life, I had to consistently fight the grip of the outer world. When mundane thoughts of worry or anxiety broke through, I had to harness my intention: rest, solitude, and silence. Even after I found illumination in the labyrinth, I itched for worldly stimulation. I distracted myself with more solitary places: gazebos, various rocking chairs, an assortment of benches, and several gardens. Even among the tall pines and a wealth of sacred tools, I struggled to keep my sabbath intention. *Wherever you go, there you are*, I reminded myself.

I returned to the rocking chair on the sidewalk behind my room and wrote in my journal. *I cannot believe I'm here. I've actually done it.* I relished the fact that I had managed to start diving into rest, solitude, and silence—even though I was terrible at it. I'd stepped away from the world to reconnect with God and replenish myself. I finally had begun to lean into sabbath as rest, but I hadn't expected the process to be so hard. I had no responsibilities at the retreat center—no laundry, no cooking, no chores, no email. My mind still swirled. So I prayed Anne Lamott style, channeling her words *help, thanks,* and *wow.*

God, help me be still. God, thanks for the time to rest, to be alone, and to be silent. God, when I rest, I can appreciate the wonder of your creation.

I'd finally managed to lull myself into a lounging posture, rocking aimlessly for thirty solid minutes, when I heard the annoying beep that all commercial trucks make when moving in reverse. I sat up in the chair, agitated. *Really, God?* I squinted my eyes to see that two football fields away in the woods a construction crew was clearing and grading land for a new home. *What the heck? How dare someone disturb my sabbath peace!* Back and forth the truck went, over and over. I tried to anticipate when it would go in reverse, soaking in the quiet seconds while it barreled forward.

Sabbath may help us get a glimpse of eternity, but it doesn't mean it will be perfect. I went back inside my cell, put in my earplugs, and took a nap. I awoke to the meal bell and gave thanks to God for a break from trying to keep sabbath rest. After lunch, I walked the outdoor trail by the dining room that was marked with the stations of the cross. I could barely hear the construction from this part of the retreat center. The afternoon stretched out before me, and I felt as if I were finally settling back into my routine of rest, solitude, and silence.

Then I heard multiple gunshots.

When I recovered from the unexpected sound, its cadence made me realize that someone was enjoying target practice and not on a homicidal mission to kill sabbatarians. The shooting went on for two hours, and the afternoon sabbath spell was *really* broken. The randomness and intensity of each ammunition round raised my blood pressure such that it was impossible to return to rest. Two weeks prior, the United States had experienced its deadliest mass shooting to date—forty-nine causalities. I was in no mood for guns, especially on a sabbath retreat.

Those who live by the sword die by the sword, I quoted to myself, remembering Jesus' warning to Peter when the disciple cut off the ear of a servant of a high priest. I became angrier with each passing minute, but my self-righteousness soon turned to defeat. *Why, Lord, why? I don't need another lesson in trying to keep sabbath amid chaos.*

I thought I'd found the perfect place to kick off my sabbath mission with lesson number one: resting. But God had something more important to teach me. No matter where I am, I will always have to contend with obstacles to sabbath—my yearning for production, my rambling mind, or someone else's idea of an afternoon well spent.

After dinner, the shooting stopped, and I'd calmed down. I walked the grounds once again, this time choosing the large meditation path that surrounds the entire retreat center. A thunderstorm rolled in five minutes later. I hurried along the trail as fast as I could, rounding its corners in a rush, the same way I'd do in the real world. When lightning cracked and I was certain my death was imminent, I came upon a cemetery with dozens of white crosses.

It was an odd graveyard with pastel-colored stones outlining the entrance. Children's figurines and statues of Mary and the saints were scattered throughout the plots, which were only two feet in length. A weathered handful of silvery birthday balloons floated up from one of the graves. Fresh flowers covered the dirt beneath it. I'd made the mistake of skimming the article on this area of the retreat center in the welcome brochure the deacon had handed me. I didn't imagine I'd actually *encounter* it during my stay. There I was, mid-thunderstorm, standing at a baby cemetery.

The resting place had been given in love and service from the retreat center's staff, who committed themselves to providing space for parents who had neither church families nor money to give their babies and toddlers a proper burial. According to the blurb, the cemetery had already reached capacity. I hurried past the balloons and heartache, running until I reached the safety of my cell. I was soaked and sad; the storm roared on.

I was the only retreatant on the entire property. One other living human was in the staff apartment seventy-five yards away, and I suddenly wished she were sleeping in the cell next to mine. I took a shower to prepare for bed and knew I'd having trouble sleeping in a new place (I always do). I'm also terrified of the dark—a completely irrational fear for an adult. I hadn't expected both to hang out in a cemetery during a monsoon and to be the *only* person on the entire property, so visions of all the horror movies I'd watched flooded my mind. Luckily, I'd brought a trinity of defense: prayer beads, pepper spray, and a nail file. I was prepared to pray, spray, and stab my way through the dark if needed.

Before crawling into the twin bed, I locked the doors to my building. I turned on every light in every room, strategically arranging mini-blind positions so that it would take a minute for an intruder to determine which one contained a terrified sabbatarian. I placed a chair in front of my door, and I borrowed another cell's chair to block the back entrance. I called Fred and my mother to tell them about the thunderstorm and my status as the next victim in a Stephen King novel. "You've got to trust in God," they both said.

I debated leaving all my belongings and running for the car. Instead, I held the prayer beads tightly and put on double eye masks to block out the light I was going to keep on all night.

Please God, keep me safe from any Stephen King characters passing through on their way to dryer weather. Please may they not have anything against Baptists or the sabbath.

I got up every fifteen minutes to check the hallway. By 1:30 a.m., I was no longer scared, just mad. Why had I let my overactive imagination steal my sabbath rest? At 2:00 a.m., I turned out the light and finally surrendered. I felt too tired to care. Four hours later, I woke up exhausted but safe, and I tried to convince myself I'd probably gotten more rest than I'd imagined. My fatigue was nothing an entire pot of coffee couldn't cure, so I staggered to breakfast, already counting the daylight hours until dusk.

Sabbath Retreat, Act II: Get Thee Behind Me, Satan

A staff member greeted me cheerfully in the dining hall. "What are you here for, sweetheart?" she asked as she poured coffee. I felt eager to dip out of my solitude and talk to someone. I told her about my sabbath exploration, and she took a seat across from me, interested. Over toast and fruit, we bemoaned the church's lack of sabbath emphasis, and together we dreamed of all the ways the body of Christ could get some rest. The impending doom of night number two seemed far away, and my retreat intention returned.

I'd begun the sabbath journey because I was physically desperate, blaming the world for its stresses and my sentence of a chronic illness. But I was beginning to understand that I was my own worst sabbath enemy. Until I learned how to surrender to God and to the tranquility of *menuchah,* I would not be able to shut out the crazy of this world and of my own mind. Day one of the sabbath retreat showed me the full extent of my struggles: my restlessness, anxiety, and fears. I stepped off the roller coaster, looking for a two-day cure-all, only to be confronted by my own baggage. Even in sacred time, my untamed mind wasn't eager to lean into the biblical mandate.

Maybe sabbath rest wasn't such good idea, I thought.

I'd already tried to monetize and maximize my retreat hours. I'd cursed construction workers just doing their jobs and wished harm on a neighbor during target practice. I didn't have faith that God would protect me through a stormy and scary night, and I couldn't subdue my mind. Exhausted, I let the Spirit have its will for how I spent my second day. *I surrender,* I said. She urged me to stay in my rocking chair and rock the day away. I did. Humility arrived.

When I hadn't been able to control my mind the prior evening, I asked my mother and Fred to pray for me. They asked me if I was praying for myself too. I realized I hadn't been consistently asking God for help in keeping sabbath. My sabbath prayers so far were more akin to what Anne Lamott calls "beggy prayers," the kind we hurl at God during airplane turbulence, even when we haven't *thought* about the Divine in two decades. I hadn't (sincerely) prayed about my sabbath practice. I'd packed academic and spiritual books on sabbath to read on retreat, but I hadn't included a stitch of scripture. It hadn't occurred to me (yet) to lean on God's Word for guidance and courage.

I spent my second morning and afternoon rocking my shame away, hoping I could do better in relying on God. I considered how sabbath was really about humility and trust, like a double portion of manna, and how I could practice "consider[ing] the lilies."

Sunset arrived, and I ended the day back at the labyrinth, where I had begun the retreat the day before. This time, I walked while acknowledging my fear of letting go of what I perceived to be control. I had been insistent on managing my own time and bridling the activities of others. I spent so much mental energy micromanaging what surrounded me that I couldn't even curb my own irrational distress in the dark. The labyrinth edge curved and pulled me inward, and I began to cry.

Why do I worry about unbridled time? Why am I spending my precious retreat time in distraction? Why am I terrified of the dark? As the circle wound tighter, an answer was laid on my heart—not an audible one—but in the mysterious language of the Spirit.

You are not relying on God for sabbath, she offered. *You are relying on yourself.*

At the center of the labyrinth, I realized the barrier I'd built against sabbath rest, solitude, and silence. I was making it all about me: my retreat, my rest, my restoration, my silence, my spiritual productivity, my break, my indispensability, my issues with control. Sabbath, instead, invites us to stop and rest in order to recalibrate to the One who is at the center. Sabbath calls us to be in awe of the Creator and Sustainer. It asks us to recognize that we can cease—and the world will go on without us—because we are humans. Sabbath reminds us that we are finite beings connected to a transcendent Creator, and when we turn toward that source, we get a glimpse of eternity.

I didn't create my tiny sphere, nor was I solely responsible for its orbit. God is in charge, and this is God's world. But when I don't stop to rest and seek solitude, my hurry, frenzy, and worry keep me from believing it. I think I'm the one who keeps all the plates spinning.

Sabbath rest is about *humility*. We aren't running the show. We *can* stop. When we do, we begin to understand that we are not the pilot but the passenger. We assert ourselves because we don't like giving up control—we want to be the masters of our own world. But God is both Creator and pilot, and until we accept that, we cannot grasp the sabbath rest instructions shared over the loudspeaker: Place your *own* oxygen mask on before assisting others. God tries to help us remember that God's got this. Who do we think we are? We ignore the sabbath commandment and neglect the very weekly practice that will enrich our lives.

Supper was quiet on the second evening. The deacon who welcomed me served, and I ate alone in silence, pondering my labyrinth epiphany over veggie lasagna. Night fell fast, and I tried to focus on God being in charge. I reluctantly returned to my building, determined not to let the day's lesson erode in darkness: Sabbath means God is in charge, not me.

No one knew this posture better than my Grandmother Evelyn, whose own sabbath insistence cost her a once-in-a-lifetime trip to the furniture market. So I asked myself, *What would Grandmother Evelyn do?*

Grandmother Evelyn certainly would not have allowed her sabbath rest to be interrupted by her own foolishness. She relied on God at every turn, and in uncertain moments, she had a special prayer at her disposal. When she sensed that she was not leaning on the everlasting arms and that she had created a tiny opening for Satan's doubt to squeeze through, she would cry, "Get thee behind me, Satan—and don't push!"

I retrieved a large metal flashlight from the desk in my room. I turned on every light in that monastic building, wielded my "sword," walked up and down the hall, and shouted, "Get thee behind me, Satan—and don't push!" I repeated the mantra over and over, hoping to ward off my fears and put God back in charge. Had the deacon been taking his evening walk and seen the commotion, I imagine he would have called for backup.

I will rely on God, I told myself. I swiped a Bible from the room adjacent to mine and settled into bed. I read Psalm 23, which my mother had taught me to do whenever I was afraid. As I switched off the light,

I reminded myself that scripture and prayer help us rely on God for life, protection, and rest.

I prayed, reciting in alphabetical order all the people, feelings, experiences, and things God—my Creator, Sustainer, and Redeemer—had provided me, ones I'm normally too busy to notice. I made it through two-and-a-half rounds of A–Z before falling asleep. Finally, I was able to place God in God's rightful place. I had nothing to fear in succumbing to rest, in being by myself, or in silence.

I got a full night's sleep.

The Gutter

The next morning, I walked the retreat center's grounds, savoring the feeling of taking a small step in my spiritual journey. I knew that a hard path lay ahead of me—intentionally trying to keep the fourth commandment each week in a world that doesn't want me to. I'd stepped away for sixty hours of rest, solitude, and silence, only to have to return to a city of nearly half a million people, my four jobs, and endless distractions.

When I took my bags to my car, I noticed a bright green plant springing up from the building's gutter. It was firmly rooted, standing tall and straight toward the sky, leaves full and proud.

How did that plant grow there? I wondered.

Gutters are icky places. They collect junk, debris, and runoff—the castaway earth and water that we don't want in our homes. *Gutter* is also a metaphor for a dirty mind or someone who lives in an undesirable place or lifestyle. These conduits are not where we typically find budding new life. Our lives are like that plant in the eaves. The world is not all bad or irredeemable. It moves quickly, like rain rushing through pipes during a storm. Even in this rough and speedy environment, growth is still possible. The seeds only need to be planted. God will feed them through water and sun—even in the gutter.

Wrestling Leads to Blessing

Though I wanted to blame culture, work, and frenzy for the reasons I couldn't rest and sit by myself in silence, my sabbath retreat made me realize that I am my own worst sabbath enemy.

Our earliest days of survival, our Puritan work ethic, and the ethos of the American Dream drive us. If we stop, who knows what thoughts and emotions might come rushing forth? But stopping—though it's frightening—is the fertile soil of spirituality. When we practice sabbath rest, solitude, and silence, we make space for growth and God's voice.

Resting in the modern age is like wrestling, but it always yields a blessing, just like Jacob's. (See Genesis 32:22-32.) Sabbath is the training ground that helps us travel the spiritual labyrinth of who we are and whose we are. After we practice sabbath rest, solitude, and silence, we re-enter the world differently.

We have all the permission we need to step away. The world will not crumble because we are neither its maker nor maintainer. We have been given a gift of time each week to rest and to be in solitude and silence in order to hear God. If we steward this gift well, we have numbered our days rightly.

Back to the Gutter

The Friday afternoon I left the retreat center, I hit traffic on the way home. Someone pulled out in front of me, and I called the driver an ugly name. Once back at my apartment, I had to reacclimate to Fred, my chores, my smartphone, and city noise. Fred and I fought for the next two days. He was stressed about a work project, and after being alone and quiet, I felt overwhelmed and overstimulated by my regular environment, which made me indecisive. I also jumped right back into work and overcommitted myself to more hours of caregiving for my mother, all while knowing I had big projects due. A steady stream of migraines began the sabbath after my retreat. By Tuesday at 1:00 p.m., while I taught my weekly weight lifting class proper dead lift form, I felt a pop, and my head exploded in pain. But I didn't stop teaching the class; I kept going and picked up the pace.

I continued to tend to my responsibilities of work, helping my mother, attending urgent meetings, and completing projects. I used my migraine rescue medications day and night for four days straight, and by Friday—a week after my retreat ended—I'd hit the maximum dosage allowed per week. I would have to wait three more days until I could take any additional medication.

I called my neurologist's office, and they insisted I come in for a blood pressure check and a migraine "cocktail" before the weekend began. With more than seventy-two hours of chronic, nonstop migraines, I was at a higher risk for a stroke. When traditional migraine medications don't work—and the migraine continues with no relief—my doctor prescribes a series of powerful injections to stop the episode immediately. These shots are potent (I would barely have time to get back to the car before passing out) and usually result in about thirty-six hours of subsequent bed rest.

When I arrived at doctor's office, my blood pressure was high.

"Do I *have* to do the shots today?" I asked, worried about not getting any work accomplished in the following days.

"Yes," she said, firmly. "I can *see* your migraine in your eyes. You have that look."

I began to cry.

Anne Lamott says that when people listen to our lament and try to understand our pain, they are holding the baby of us. Chronic migraine is so misunderstood; there are no blood tests or x-rays to "prove" to people how I feel. Migraineurs must rely on the empathy of doctors, spouses, family members, friends, and supervisors who *believe* them when they describe their symptoms. When my doctor said she could *see* my migraine, I felt understood. I followed her directions.

My doctor insisted on the shots *and* a cortisone steroid taper beginning the next day should I have even a twinge of head pain. It was only the second time in my life I'd had the injections, and the first time she'd also given me a cortisone taper. Fred and I remembered when I'd received the shots four years prior. We knew we had about a five-minute window before I became dizzy, confused, and, ultimately, passed out.

I was delayed leaving the neurologist's office, and Fred rushed me to the car, lying me down in the passenger seat just in time. After singing a brief chorus of "Silent Night, Holy Night," I was asleep before he pulled out of the parking lot. He drove me home and got me in bed, and I slept until noon the next day, began cortisone, and was finally freed from the nearly weeklong migraine by the time the Sunday sabbath arrived.

My sabbath retreat felt far away, and I realized that two days' worth of practice was not going to hold me over for a lifetime. A booster shot of sabbath can't shield me from the world. That's the beauty of the sabbath design; it's comes around *weekly*, so that, when executed properly and consistently, the practice spills over into regular time. I couldn't complete one silent retreat and expect to have permanent immunity from life's demands. I had to give my full heart to sabbath one day per week, allowing it to transform and inform the other six days.

After the migraine incident, I started a weekly practice of sabbath rest, solitude, and silence. Slowly, it helped me weed out the extraneous pressures and tasks I was taking on. I gained sabbath perspective: I don't need to fill every minute with an activity. I don't need to check my phone or email every five minutes. Instead, I need to take a nap; I need to sit in silence and pray; I need to seek space for listening to God. Sabbath rest is a continual exploration, and it only happens when I let go and lean into God. True sabbath rest is infused with the humility to surrender to the "palace of time" and to accept God's generous gift.

6

SABBATH AS WORSHIP

Some keep the Sabbath going to Church—
I keep it, staying at Home
—EMILY DICKINSON

When we think of sabbath as worship, we often find ourselves succumbing to church boredom disease. Symptoms include daydreaming during the scripture reading, doodling away anthems, and sleeping through sermons. Announcements might be the only known cure, sparking a feverish reading of the bulletin—twice—making certain we don't miss out on any church happenings. At the end of the hour, when pewmates begin texting their friends about lunch plans and some old man's digital watch alerts us of the noon hour, everyone is relieved. The illness is staved off for another week. Worshiping inside a church is not always what we'd like to be doing on the sabbath. Even Emily Dickinson wasn't fond of it.

Year after year, Americans lose more interest in the institutional church—even those who identify as serious Christians. Worship services (devotional hymns, sacred readings, inspirational sermons) no longer seem to draw crowds, and attending church feels like it takes up half of our day off. So we stop going completely.

Church is no longer an American mainstay. Centuries—even decades ago—people counted on worship to replenish them in both good and tough times (wars, disease outbreaks, economic depressions, and the threat of nuclear weaponry). Services might be tedious, but it was also a centering experience embedded in society. Today, when we do manage to darken the parish doorstep, we run to our cars at noon, wondering if we even got anything out of the eleven o'clock hour.

I Don't Need No Church

I once heard a sermon on the importance of attending worship. The preacher shared his frustration about those who wanted nothing to do with a structured, communal service of devotional practice in a sacred space.

"But God is everywhere," people would tell him. "Why would I need to go to church?"

"God *is* everywhere," the preacher agreed. "But when's the last time you acted like it?"

We claim we are rooted in Jesus' teachings, and we don't need church to remind us of it. But worship—whether practiced in a church, temple, synagogue, house, school cafeteria, or park—serves a purpose. During the week, we remain siloed, distracted by our own worries and obligations. We may try to operate under the belief that God is present and in control, but we often forget. We're not connected and thoughtful; we behave in ways that we would never dream of acting in a sacred space.

Communal praise and devotion is not about hypocrisy—acting one way on Sunday and living another way Monday through Saturday; it's about reinforcement and reminders. Holy spaces offer opportunities to be focused on *devotion*—acknowledging the Divine, giving thanks, confessing our shortcomings, and turning to God—in a way that shapes us the rest of the week. This time spent in communal worship is like exercising: It strengthens us and makes us accountable to God and to others. In worship, we gain gospel muscle memory for the week.

Nature Deficit Disorder

The April sun was already hot. Infant leaves shimmied in lime-green splendor, and the grass was flattened underneath our lawn chairs. Nature put on her Sunday best for the first-annual Binkley Baptist Church Earth Day worship service. Handbells and birds offered the call and response, and the soon-to-be dedicated Holy Spirit dove sculpture twirled on its pedestal. For the first time in my life, I attended an entire Sunday worship service outside.

The sermon began with Emily Dickinson's poem "Some keep the Sabbath going to Church." The Victorian poet describes her rebellious calling not to spend Sundays in the pews but out among flying creatures and orchards. God is Dickinson's clergyman, and his sermons are short. Perhaps Dickinson foresaw American's future widespread aversion to church.

Nearly seventy years ago in the South, church was the hub from which culture and social lives radiated—sometimes to the detriment of progress but other times anchoring us to our purpose in Christ. Now, work, busyness, and social media have become the well from which we draw our weekly sustenance—and even activism.[1] We practice alternative forms of worship: holy hikes and brunch benedictions. This is what made Binkley Church's first open-air Sunday a game-changer. Worshiping outdoors was not only a testimonial to Binkley Church's commitment to be "conscientious caretakers of the earth," a line from the church covenant, but also a brilliant move to draw those who might otherwise play church-hooky on a sunny, seventy-degree spring day.

This alfresco Earth Day church service signified Binkley's protest of the Anthropocene age. The church had just added solar panels to its roof and committed to sustainable landscaping. Its grounds were certified as a nature reserve, and a Community Supported Agriculture (CSA) program began operating out of the building. Celebrating God's hand in these feats was the kind of twenty-first-century worship service everyone could get behind.

Binkley's front lawn was covered that day—perhaps with the largest intergenerational crowd I'd seen in a long while on a Sunday morning. Teenagers lounged on blankets, babies cried, Boomers blocked the sun with bulletins, and octogenarians nearly melted. We'd shed our typical formalities, clapping at musical revelations and fanning ourselves in camping chairs. It felt less churchy and more like a music festival, something I don't think Jesus would have minded with his dusty feet and penchant for outdoor preaching. We'd forgone the Freon in favor of worship in *creation*. I felt closer to the sacred text and nearer to the first sabbath when God, having completed God's work of creating the earth and all the beings, rested. *This is what the American Christian church needs,* I thought.

Many of us toil indoors all week, a far cry from our agricultural ancestors. We suffer from Nature Deficit Disorder, a condition not yet worthy of medical coding but real nonetheless. Worshiping in nature solves two problems: (1) the modern yearning for being outdoors and (2) the longing to praise God while doing it.

I found absorbing liturgy and lessons amid fresh dew on fuchsia flowers so much easier. I was full of praise and awe and devotion, finally experiencing the "thin space" Celtic spirituality describes. God's glory felt as close as the nesting birds and restless toddlers.

Why weren't we worshiping like this more often?

The Church's One Foundation

I don't recall Baptists singing "The Church's One Foundation" when I was growing up. Perhaps it was too much talk of unification, oneness, and avoiding schisms. Baptists don't fret over division; we love an excuse to show off our local church autonomy.

I earned my seminary education at Duke Divinity School, which was filled with Methodists, whose "method" is consistency across a connectional system. Their churches are anchored by the weekly lectionary, their Book of Discipline, district superintendents, and bishops. Even amid such homogeny, there are still differing opinions about what one should (and shouldn't) do during the worship hour. Methodists, who pride themselves on unification "mid toil and tribulation" take on the characteristics of their Baptist cousins when it comes to the Lord's Day. And if the equanimous

Methodists disagree on how to remember the sabbath and keep it holy, the rest of us are really in trouble.

I didn't realize some Methodists hold differing views on the practical aspects of sabbath-keeping until I shared breakfast with a certified lay leader who expressed concerns about her denomination's lack of interest in certain sabbath practices. I had assumed that only Baptists fought about *everything* and that our Protestant cousins had a tidy checklist somewhere on the dos and don'ts of sabbath worship. How Methodists handle *contemplative* worship practices on the sabbath, it seems, varies.

"People look at me like I'm crazy when I talk about the time I spend discerning God's voice in silence," the lay leader confided. "How can we listen to God if we aren't silent?" Her voice faltered. When she'd encouraged her church to reserve some Sunday worship time for *listening* for the voice of God in the quiet, she had received pushback. "Why is listening not a priority?" she asked.

I had heard these same concerns from young adults, seniors, families with children, and fellow clergy from many Protestant denominations. Most everyone I talked to had some idea of sabbath including worship, but nearly everyone disagreed on how to show our devotion. Should worship be just one hour? How much contemplative or silent time should be included? Should the service have more of a coffee-hour, concert-hall, revival-tent-meeting feel or have a monastic ambiance? Should we sing traditional or contemporary music? Should we use screens or bulletins? Do we need a drummer or an organist? Outlining *how* to praise God has gotten as noisy as any other hot-button church issue.

"We even have *meetings* on Sunday," the lay leader added. "I don't think the church *really* wants us to have a sabbath." She longed for her church to use Sunday as a day to refuel, but the church had to conduct its business. I'd heard other parishioners offer a similar disdain for committee recruitment and tasks when they attended worship. The church was beginning to look at lot like work with folks sneaking out the back door—or not coming at all—for fear of getting tapped. When we program ourselves to death at church, we don't leave much space for offering praise, giving thanks, and listening for God.

The body of Christ is extremely gifted at outreach—evangelism and missions—but it often neglects the *internal* process of Christianity. Services on the spiritual practices of contemplative prayer, Taizé, and healing only occur a few times a year. The remainder of the liturgical seasons' worship hours are spent with pastors and choir directors trying to keep us awake and amused, competing with gurgling stomachs and the smartphones in everyone's lap.

The church is also guilty of using the worship hour to perpetuate the call to exhaustion: "Join our forty-five committees!" "Don't forget to come to all twelve programs this week!" "Need another full-time job? The church has got your back!" Visitors are even recruited and overwhelmed—perhaps even on their first Sunday in attendance.

The church's intention is certainly pure—bishops and pastors and music ministers and spiritual formation leaders want to maximize worship services as an opportunity for folks to find places to plug in and build community. But church can quickly turn into a long list of to-dos, and sabbath worship begins to feel anything but sacred. We've lost sight of the church's one foundation—which is Jesus Christ her Lord—and we, her stewards, are too busy to notice.

Church, Interrupted

In 2008, the Rev. Kara Root became the pastor of Lake Nokomis Presbyterian Church, a declining congregation in need of respite. Like many small American parishes, her congregation boasted only thirty regular Sunday worship attendees. The budget and operations had shrunk, and the church was in danger of closing its doors within two years. But Rev. Root and her flock turned her worshiping community around with one change: sabbath.[2]

Desperation led to opportunity, and Root saw an opening to adjust her church's worship calendar. With her parishioners' support, she established a new monthly schedule that mirrored a biblical sabbath rhythm. She led traditional worship services on the first and third Sundays of the month, and on the second and fourth Sundays, everyone was off. There was no worship hour those days, which meant that parishioners were free to take an entire day of rest, solitude, silence, prayer, study, and community on their own—with no guilt of missing services. On the occasional fifth Sunday, everyone participated in a service project.

This new church pattern freed members from any mental or physical obligation to attend worship *every* Sunday. For those who insisted they still needed a structured, guided weekly service, Root offered Saturday evening contemplative services, reflecting on the previous Sunday's texts and sermon. The result? Lake Nokomis Presbyterian Church's worship attendance is up.

The church now has ninety members; forty to seventy attend the bimonthly Sunday services up from its meager thirty. Twelve to twenty-five people frequent the Saturday night contemplative gatherings. Since implementing the new worship schedule, families with young children have joined, and the church's budget has received a much-needed infusion.

By returning to observing an ancient rhythm of sabbath-as-worship and also encouraging congregants to engage in rest, solitude, silence, and community, Rev. Root discovered the very thing the church needed to save itself. How might other clergy realize this for themselves, as well as convince their parishioners, that doing less is doing more?

Clergy Sabbath-Keepers

Reverend Root successfully taught her congregation how to observe sabbath in a contemporary age. But most clergy find sabbath discussions to be an uphill battle—one they don't address much. I interviewed clergy of all ages, persuasions, and denominations about sabbath practices. They agreed to share their feedback anonymously, as they have very different understandings of their personal sabbath practices in comparison to that which they recommend for their flock. I was surprised by their responses.

For one of my dearest clergy friends, who pastors an aging church in an urban setting, sabbath is a Tuesday afternoon matinee. Her "worship" hour has nothing to do with Jesus or scripture or the church. Rather, this kind of sabbath allows her a release from what is her ordinary, everyday

time: religious work. She said she loved the experience of something
non-church as sabbath, like an afternoon of imaginative delight in a cool,
dark place.

As leaders of faith communities, the clergy I spoke with know the
importance of—and their own lack of—sabbath practices. They've studied the sabbath texts and its praxis in seminary classrooms. They know
how to construct a theologically sound worship service and encourage
community. After decades of preaching the lectionary, they can teach
complex parables with their eyes closed. But even for them, insisting on
and modeling the six-and-one rhythm of stopping, ceasing, praising, and
serving escapes their grasp. They are overworked and underappreciated,
taken for granted in a chosen vocational circumstance that Duke Divinity
School professor Stanley Hauerwas once described as being "nibbled to
death by ducks."[3]

It's hard for ministers to model sabbath when everyone is wearing
them out. The ones I surveyed (from different generations, experience
levels, races, and parish settings) met my sabbath questions with some
sadness and frustration. It's not that they don't cherish the importance of
sabbath; in fact, they crave it for themselves and others. They have faith
in its restorative powers. But they, like their parishioners, feel the pull of
everyone vying for their time.

Sundays are workdays for clergy, so their sabbaths must be observed
on another day of the week. Most designate Fridays or Mondays, but they
struggle to protect that time. Adding sabbath to a minister's calendar
doesn't prevent a church member from dying or having major surgery.
Instead, pastors I spoke with grab a half-day when they can, often engaging in non-church activities (church, after all, is their everyday experience) that the rest of us might find surprising, like going to the movies
or composing music at their favorite coffee shop. Still, clergy sabbath is
rare; committee meetings pop up, emergencies arise, and ministers feel
that they are on call for their flock 24/7, especially if their churches are
short-staffed.

Many say that an entire day of sabbath as rest, worship, and community is nearly impossible for them. They may not be saying enough about

sabbath from the pulpit because it's so difficult for them to model it when they can barely dip into the practice themselves. Clergy are also weekend-workers, which means they understand the complexity of laboring in an economy where many Americans work Saturday and Sunday shifts. This may be why they are less vocal about sabbath observance than new converts like Kate Rademacher would like them to be.

But clergy work hard amid all their pastoral care responsibilities to design meaningful sabbath worship services most of us would rather skip. We, the parishioners, must also be mindful that we are guilty of being boundary-sucking vipers who play hooky from church and then complain that our pastors aren't doing enough for *us*. We must remember that the worship hour is both the culmination and continuation of a week's worth of labor for pastors. While some congregants live for this weekly tune-up, others avoid it all together.

The one thing that pastors *and* parishioners agree on when it comes to sabbath is that *everyone* is skeptical about finding a total of twenty-four hours of *menuchah* in a nonstop world. Clergy and laypersons both realize that amid our complex faith communities and work/family obligations, a day's worth of sabbath observance doesn't feel realistic. Nearly every minister I asked believes that modern American culture and economics prevent us from designating a single day for rest, worship, and community. They don't think that's going to change. The days of slow, country sabbaths like the ones my mother and her siblings enjoyed—and the ones I cherished in Dana and Reidsville—are gone. But that doesn't mean the need isn't there.

Pastors are compassionate helpers; they respect personalities, seasons of life, and needs for autonomy in the sabbath experience. They are mindful of many tugs on their diverse flock. While they hope sabbath can be purposeful—filled with devotion, scripture study, solitude, rest, or gathered community—they also know that people may seek their weekly renewal elsewhere.

Some clergy attempt to teach us about sabbath. They offer Bible studies and sermon series. But when parishioners do attend church, pastors don't want them to feel shamed or punished for not embodying a particular practice. They are resistant to drive the sabbath message home as passionately as they might baptism or Communion because it's difficult to instruct others on a subject they haven't yet wrangled themselves.

But we *need* clergy to model sabbath-keeping for us, particularly with regard to worship. Whether it's holding services outside, including moments of sanctuary contemplation, or even taking a Sunday off from worship, we need communal devotional practice to calm the noise around us.

Parishioners must remember too that sabbath as worship is a team sport, requiring both clergy and congregants to be devoted *together*. Whether we are in the hallowed halls of an ancient cathedral, in a bowling-alley-turned-Baptist church, or in the quiet of the parish gardens, worshiping God is an essential part of keeping sabbath holy.

7

SABBATH AS COMMUNITY

"Where two or three are gathered in my name, I am there among them."
—MATTHEW 18:20

In her 2005 *Christian Century* essay, pastor and professor Barbara Brown Taylor outlines her personal journey and struggle with creating a sabbath-keeping practice. Though she had successfully established a weekly "practice of eternal life," something was still missing: the fact that she did it alone.[1]

Sabbath observed as rest, solitude, and silence is certainly a necessary portion of the fourth commandment. It's one way Jesus observed it. Sabbath practiced individually has many benefits, including listening for and communing with God. But Taylor sees her growth edge (and the church's) as keeping sabbath *together.*

"God did not give this commandment to a person but to a people, knowing that only those who rested together would be equipped to resist together."[2] Keeping sabbath not only prevents our own exhaustion but also defends against the exploitation of others. If a Christian or Jew truly believes in the Abrahamic God (and thus keeps sabbath), the fourth commandment insists that he or she also give a day off to anyone who works for him or her. (See Exodus 20:10.) In this way, sabbatarians don't take advantage of others by benefitting economically or culturally from someone else working while they rest.

Real sabbath, Taylor insists, is done in community each week and every seven years, Leviticus 25-style. Everyone and everything is affected: land and animals are given rest; debts are forgiven; those who work in bondage (literally or metaphorically) are freed. It's the kind of wild community cooperation we've come to expect from a triune God. Traditional order is turned upside down; the rules of the game are changed.

But such a radical interweaving of community dependence will not arrive in a church that has too much invested in benefitting from capitalism. Resistance as a community, Taylor insists, comes from those who remove themselves from the merry-go-round. When we remember the sabbath, we remember that we are made in God's image. Taylor writes that this facet of who we are leads us to join God in the "holy work of mending the world."[3]

Modern theologians like Barbara Brown Taylor and Walter Brueggemann are fervent in their call to us: Sabbath-keeping is nearly impossible to practice in isolation. Yes, there's room for solitude, but if we want our world, culture, work, economy, lives, and time to be transformed by sabbath, we must begin in our communities.

Called to Community

If the practice of sabbath was created during God's final act of Creation, it must call for a creation-wide effort. But we know the modern church's lack of guidelines on sabbath praxis causes both veteran church members as well as eager converts, like Kate Rademacher, to not know what to do with the fourth commandment.

Outside of Judaism, Seventh-day Adventists, and the Church of Jesus Christ of Latter Day Saints, community-wide doctrine on sabbath does not exist. Christians practice sabbath (or don't practice) as individuals, families, or in isolated worship hours, which can lead to complacency. Let's face it: None of us is that good at accountability. Ask anyone who's ever tried a fad diet or started a New Year's resolution exercise program.

The self-discipline it takes to make sabbath a well-rounded practice of rest, worship, and community requires the community.

The Upper Room

Jesus was a sabbatarian. He valued time alone in prayer, he worshiped and studied in the temple, and he was *really* into community. Jesus managed to recruit followers to journey and teach with him, and he even kept the sustained attention of the hungry five thousand. During community time, he preached, taught, healed, and offered rituals and instructions on what folks should do when they gather together.

On what Christians now observe as Maundy Thursday, Jesus rallied his friends for a communal meal that would eventually morph into the early church's sacrament of Eucharist—or Communion. We know this community meal, which occurred in the upper room, is important because it shows up in all four Gospels and in the first letter to the Corinthians. (See Matthew 26:26-29; Mark 14:22-25; Luke 22:17-20; John 14:1-4; 1 Corinthians 11:23-26.)

From the early first century to today, Eucharist remains the church's only institutionalized sabbath custom of remembering Jesus' ministry, death, and resurrection. The account of the Last Supper in the Gospel of John focuses less on the meal (it only mentions that it happened) and more on the theology of what is yet to come and how to handle it—together. After Jesus washes his disciples' feet, he offers a dense sermon (called the "Farewell Discourse"), which spans four chapters. (See John 14–17.) He preaches betrayal, denial, comfort, discipleship, and love—all lessons for how to act (or not act) in community. Jesus knows that this particular gathering of the disciples will never happen in the same way again. When he sees them again, things will be *very* different.

The next time Jesus' students share space with him, one student has betrayed him. Others have run away, and one has committed suicide. When Christ appears to the disciples after his death, they are in gathered community, but this time they are grieving and wrestling with his perplexing teachings.

The Ladies Man: A Lesson in Community

Tim Meadows is a comedian known for his 90s *Saturday Night Live* character, "The Ladies Man." When Meadows came to Goodnight's Comedy Club in Raleigh, Fred and I attended our first and only stand-up comedy show. It was just as I expected: bawdy, obvious, and filled with self-deprecating humor.

Meadows moved through his bits deliberately while his audience waited for what they'd really come for: his "Ladies Man" impression. But mid-set, when I felt bored and longed for the lisp of the exaggerated SNL stud, Meadows paused soberly and said, "Do you realize that we will all never be in this space, at this time, with these people ever again?"

Nervous laughter ensued. Was he setting up a joke?

It was an odd detour, and Meadows stepped away from it as quickly as he had gotten in, reading cues that no one was up for philosophical ponderings. But I was transfixed. As someone who does community professionally—and who studied its theological meaning in the hallowed halls of Duke—I'd never reached the conclusion he just shared: Community is ever-changing. It's up to us to notice when it happens. There I was among strangers and chicken wings, having an existential crisis in a comedy bar. Meadows eventually got to the "Ladies Man," but I couldn't stop thinking about community.

After that night, I couldn't escape the reality that community is fluid. At baseball games, birthday parties, funerals, and worship services, I was smacked by Meadows's revelation that no two moments in community are identical. Nothing can be replicated, and so each gathering becomes a radical call to live in the present—like Jesus did.

Raised in the Baptist church, I'd always taken community for granted. The Baptists were perpetually getting together: gathering for Sunday school, worship, Bible study, youth group, handbells, choirs, potlucks, Friday night high school football parties, mission trips, and ski weekends. I'd never realized that even as we spent so much time together, the dynamics constantly shifted. We were growing and changing as teens and as a youth group—formed by our time with one another.

In all my years in church, seminary, and as a student of the Last Supper, I'd never put this together.

That night at a comedy club, I learned an important theological lesson from a TV character. Sabbath revelation, it seems, arrives when we least expect it.

Over-Deviled Eggs and Burnt Chicken

In the over-programmed era of the twenty-first century, which stands in sharp contrast to my smartphone-free youth of the 1990s, churches are guilty of overdoing. Our bulletins are filled with events, committee meetings, potlucks, and small groups. We are one CorningWare dish away from running for the exit, screaming, "Ugh. *Community*. Not again!"

But communal, shared meals—with no agenda or achievable goals—are few and far between. While serving my second term as a deacon at Binkley Baptist, I discovered that time spent eating together—the simplest and most accessible form of community in our culture—is rare. While scheduling my biannual post-worship lunch with fifteen of the church's families whom I care for, the date had to be changed *three* times before we eventually had to cancel. And it wasn't the parishioners' schedules that posed a problem; it was the church calendar. Every Sunday we picked to share our meal interfered with a last-minute church-wide activity that (appropriately) took priority over my rinky-dink potluck. If our church calendars are as full as our Google calendars, then finding a time to even have a meal together becomes a chore.

The twentieth-century allure of the post-church potluck hasn't retained its appeal. Families have places to go and errands to run. Churches have responded with different kinds of community programing, usually bigger and better—like large-scale, parking-lot sized events with inflatable slides and snow cone machines. "Theology on Tap" and "Beer and Hymns" has also gained traction among Millennial Christians, as desperate churches try to find ways to attract and gather young people. But even these bits of community, which are well-meaning and cleverly themed, can feel more like happy hour and less like sabbath.

The Cost

What does it cost us to skip the practice of community, especially as it relates to sabbath? Studies at Cornell University's School of Industrial and Labor Relations found that people who are pressured to work overtime and spend less time in community—in any form—suffer higher rates of severe conflict, alcoholism, stress, and absenteeism.[4] We know we *need* one another, just as the latest fascination with the *Friends* TV show suggests, but because every other moment of our lives is programmed, we run out of steam for the practice that should come first.

Christians who long for rest, devotional time, and close relationships often lack the guidance, support, and accountability of sabbath-keeping. Some individuals may not even know what they need. Rabbi Arthur Waskow, director of the Shalom Center, writes that religious communities have a duty to wake up and intercede. Waskow wrote the "Free Time/Free People" interfaith statement, a polemic that demonstrates how religious communities can be intentional and instrumental in helping their flocks practice a well-rounded sabbath.

When faith communities commit to sabbath practices as a community, they become allies for themselves, families, and workers. Houses of worship that are purposeful in designing meaningful gatherings that provide structure and inspiration for their congregants to practice rest, worship, and community help them be happier and more productive during the workweek.

The "Free Time/Free People" statement, put together by the Shalom Center, is a call to utilize community time to encourage political, economic, and cultural leaders to model and emphasize more free time spent with worshiping communities, family, and friends.[5] Signers included Tony Campolo, the Rev. Jesse Jackson, Rabbi Michael Lerner, Cornel West, and the editors of *Sojourners*. The statement reinforced the idea that religious communities' sabbath *can* influence culture, economics, and relationships. When faith communities offer sabbath structure and support to protect the gifts of Creation, they also enter the public policy arena and help facilitate change.

Scholar Dorothy Bass writes that practicing sabbath in community fosters resilience against the distorted ways we live out our other days. Sabbath in community becomes countereconomic, countercultural, and countertemporal. Bass isn't saying that we should hearken back to legalistic sabbaths and fearing idleness; rather, Bass believes in sabbath imperfection—which actually reinforces our reliance upon God's grace.[6] Christians especially are called to share a sabbath practice as the body of Christ so that we can impact how we operate in and for the world. She insists that religious communities can and should stand up for weekday economics that lead to sabbath community ethics: livable hours, living wages, and the right to rest and reconnect with God and family. Bass reminds us that sabbath forms and nurtures both the individual and the community distinctly, such that it "foster[s] a way of being in the world that spills over to affect an entire way of life."[7]

No matter how or why Christians arrive at sabbath community—exhaustion, curiosity, longing, or a mandate—Bass insists that sabbath is a social endeavor. Even in rest, solitude, and silence, we learn from watching and imitating one another.

The American ethos of individualism is counter to being a part of, obedient to, and vulnerable to gathered community. We are less aware of our reliance upon one another for daily living. This manifests in our disconnection from agriculture and how goods arrive at stores (or our doorstep). Our personhood is reinforced in our selfie culture. Amazon reminds us of our individualistic purchasing power. We consistently think of our own personal progress (achieving and acquiring) rather than our role in striving for the greater good of community. But there is an alternative, and it's found in community. When the body of Christ practices sabbath through gathering, our lives both inside and outside the church are informed. Who (and whose) we are becomes more apparent in the world.

Life Together

Dietrich Bonhoeffer, twentieth-century theologian and Lutheran pastor, wrote extensively on community and discipleship. Bonhoeffer, who was imprisoned during WWII for his opposition to Nazism, believed that our primary purpose in life is to discover who we already are: We are made in the image of God and called to do God's work—even if, like Jesus, we are faced with violence and death.

A contemporary reading of Bonhoeffer reminds us that Jesus taught his first-century followers that he had come so that they might have life abundantly (John 10:10)—but not in the material sense. Jesus wanted to instill that status and stuff don't yield a meaningful existence. The more we resist who we are as spiritual creatures, the more restless we feel. The gospel calls us to a great consciousness that can only be found in contemplating and embodying who we really are—*together*, in community.[8]

Bonhoeffer was the ultimate example of how being tuned into our truest identities helps us follow Jesus' teachings in community. He sacrificed a prestigious American academic career to return to his native Germany to be a voice against Jewish persecution and a force against Nazi powers. He paid a steep price for his resistance; he died for his faith in the face of injustice.

Even when Bonhoeffer was imprisoned, he continued to speak out and build community *behind* bars, teaching and ministering to his fellow prisoners. He was eventually sentenced to death by hanging, just eleven days before the liberation of the concentration camp where he'd been kept.[9] Prior to his execution, his last communal act was to share the liturgy of the Lord's Supper with his prison community, during which it is said that his final words were, "This is the end, for me the beginning of life."[10]

We are all not called to such extreme sacrifices as the ones Bonhoeffer made, but we, as Christians, are called to build and sustain community no matter where we are. Sabbath offers us a weekly opportunity to do just that.

It Takes a Village

A few years ago, my best friend, Kate, and her husband, Jim, held a camping-themed birthday party for their firstborn, Wesley. He was turning two on an uncharacteristically warm Saturday in February, the kind of midwinter reprieve North Carolina is so good at. As the toddler and his friends teetered around the yard, his mother and I watched him from the kitchen sink.

Look at this boy's community, I thought. *He has all of us: his blood relatives but also me and Fred, his surrogate aunt and uncle, who have adored him since before he was born.*

I thought about his future, picturing his eighteenth birthday when I might stand at the same sink with his mother, wondering where the time went but still amazed by the tribe who loved and nurtured him since he was in the womb. This community—those people gathered on that February day—will remain with Wesley his entire life, whether we are physically present or just a memory.

The same goes for the children at church. In the Baptist tradition, in lieu of infant baptism, we hold baby dedications. In this ritual, the pastor brings the parents, relatives, and child to the front of the congregation. We, the child's community, make promises. We covenant to assist the family members in raising their child in the light and love of the church.

In this way, we all become family, loving one another through good times and bad. We look out for the child. We guide and teach her in Sunday school; we take him on youth trips. We listen when the child becomes an angry teen and feels she cannot go to her parents with her problems. These sabbaths, when we all commit to raising this precious child, restore my hope in community.

These dedication Sundays suggests that our unity through Christ is really what makes us family, not blood-ties or surnames. It echoes Jesus' message of community—"Where two or three are gathered in my name, I am there with them" (Matt. 18:20)—and later Paul's metaphor for parts of the body as the body of Christ—"The body does not consist of one member but of many" (1 Cor. 12:14).

The Kitchen Table

I have an odd nuclear family configuration. My only sibling is eighteen years older than I am, and he was already working as a doctor by the time

I was nine years old. My brother, mother, and a slew of grandparents, aunts, uncles, and older cousins helped raised me. But we didn't gather for shared meals the way my mother's generation had. By the time I was born, I knew they loved and supported me, but they were also off doing their own thing, raising children and just trying to survive.

I often wondered what it would be like to have a giant Sunday table full of siblings and conversations, the way I imagined my mother's childhood had been since she was the youngest of five. I envision it having the same charm and light as a Thomas Kinkade painting, but I know real families don't function that way.

Western culture has a concept of family of origin versus family of choice. The patching together of modern "families" is often a mixture of blood, kin, adoptive relatives, and friends. It's precisely the kind of "body" Paul writes about in First Corinthians: "In the one Spirit we were all baptized into one body—Jews or Greeks, slaves or free" (12:13).

Last March, Fred and I were invited to celebrate the fortieth birthday of our dear friend Heather. We went to her best friend's home to gather with a family we'd never met. Work colleagues joined us, in-laws arrived, and two hours into the party, we were sitting at a sturdy kitchen table with a beautiful mishmash of the birthday girl's tribe. Fred and I stayed at that table all night, laughing and talking with folks we'd just met about politics, religion, careers, caregiving, dating, and cars.

The spring evening turned to darkness; time flowed effortlessly, just like it had at Susan's Passover Seder. The clock ticked, but Fred and I were totally engrossed in conversation. By then, I'd learned the lesson Tim Meadows and Jesus had taught me: We cannot recreate this evening—ever. That night represented sabbath as community to me—time spent completely immersed with others.

It's no coincidence that the kitchen is always the heart of the home. No matter how much square footage we own or rent, whether we have a commercial or galley kitchen, folks are drawn to the center that feeds us—literally and figuratively. Jesus didn't miss that memo. He gathered his best friends at a large table over a simple, communal meal. When I'm paying attention, I see glimpses of that upper room on the sabbath in my deacon family lunch, birthday parties, homemade dinners with our closest friends, my college-aged cousins, or impromptu cookouts with neighbors.

Church grounds us in a community that worships a baby born to poor parents. He became a mendicant preacher who taught us that we can get a glimpse of eternity in and through community. Sabbath as community arrives when we find ourselves sitting with one another in shared awe and wonder, marveling at what it means to be present. It is then that we connect ourselves to the divine mystery of sabbath, when God showed us how to cease from our work in order to actually enjoy creation—*together*.

8

My Sabbath Journey
(What I've Learned
So Far)

This isn't a contest but the doorway into thanks.
—Mary Oliver, "Praying"

Americans want to be the best at everything. Our culture has boiled success down to a science. We know the number of hours it takes to master a craft (10,000) and how to achieve our milestones through goals and good old-fashioned grit. We make our mark on this world through ambition that leads to legacy and material goods that yield status. But when we apply this kind of thinking to sabbath, we get in trouble. The "Go big or go home" mentality sets us up to fail. We worry that if we can't observe the fourth commandment in its fullest sense, we should give up entirely.

The Japanese have a lovely antidote for this kind of self-sabotage. *Wabi-sabi* is the acceptance of imperfection and impermanence. When applied to sabbath, *wabi-sabi* is the idea that we should strive for keeping the sabbath with some levity. It's not that we don't take sabbath seriously;

rather, we accept the difficulty inherent in reserving an entire day for rest, worship, and community in a culture and economy that doesn't want us to.

There are real barriers to sabbath. Privilege is a major one. How can a person who is working three minimum-wage jobs, not making ends meet, and barely providing for children even think about a day off? But even people who have the socioeconomic ability *not* to work seven days per week experience blocks to sabbath.

There is grace, but it doesn't mean letting ourselves off the hook completely. John Wesley's doctrine of perfection is a good reminder of this. We've all been given the tools to create a fuller life. We only have to use them with humility and a touch of discipline.

Remembering to step outside of our daily lives to rest, worship, or gather for a day or an entire afternoon puts us in a posture of awe and appreciation. It's our weekly calendar reminder that we are not in charge and we don't control the universe, contrary to what our constant swiping and liking leads us to believe.

Practicing sabbath turns our worlds upside down and requires us to ask: *How do we gain something by doing nothing? How do refill ourselves by emptying?*

It's the Journey, Not the Destination

My sabbath journey stemmed from my physical desperation of chronic migraine and my struggles to alleviate stress in order to experience the fullness of life. Had I not had a health crisis or gotten fed up with my own whining, I might not have accepted the Spirit's invitation to revisit ancient medicine to cure my modern woes.

There is often an inciting incident that slows us down and calls us to sabbath, whether we recognize it or not. It's something that knocks us off our track, a signal to stress less—or else—and to depend upon something that transcends us. But we don't need a crisis to get into this club.

My sabbath journey began when the practice came easily—from singing, "Saraluia! I thank you, Lord!" to gushing over youth group boys. I was told to keep the sabbath and obliged, but I never knew why I did it.

It's the *why* of a thing that keeps it relevant, which is the reason I dropped the sabbath-as-joy habit as soon as I hit college.

The need to ask *why* arrived nearly twenty years later, thanks to a Q-tip and a chronic disease that required Botox for its remission. But there's no need to wait until the quartet accompanies our sinking Titanic. Getting to the crux of sabbath will rescue us before we drown.

The Road Less Traveled

My exploration of the history of a tradition unique to the Judeo-Christian religions grounded me in the *why*. I learned about sabbath's scriptural basis, its meaning for the enslaved Hebrews, and how sabbath informed Jesus and the early church. The shift from Saturday to Sunday for the newly-minted Christianity made sense, but its symbolism and meaning got lost in the prudishness of long church hours and a loss of wonder.

Now, our tech culture makes even members of Generation Z, who have never lived without cell phones, miss the "good ol' days." But we can step off the crazy-train and re-enter the "palace in time." We only have to rest, worship, and seek community—but it won't be a popular path. In a year of experimenting with sabbath-keeping, I have failed, made mistakes, and asked for grace.

Resting means confronting the itchiness of wanting to keep our bodies (and minds) moving. Worship means finding a place in which we can really concentrate on devotion—and it's amazing how much we (myself included) are unwilling to sacrifice an hour to spend in God's house. Community means stepping out of comfort zones to risk rejection and navigate complex relationship dynamics in order to spend quality time together—whether it's over dinner or in service to a greater good.

It's no mystery why we want to skip the "work" of sabbath, but the dividends abound. My eyes have been opened to my culture, its pace, and the privilege of having a day off. I now know how it feels to be silent and by myself for two days—and how that's when the my fears and insecurities come out to play. Most of all, I've been reintroduced to humility—the idea that I am not the center of the universe. And the act of yielding to

God (who's in charge, by the way) means I have recognized this fact. In some ways, not keeping sabbath is about ego.

We can easily intellectualize sabbath, but we still need to get to the nuts and bolts. How are we called to resist our culture and economy in favor of wonder and service? We will always face obstacles to sabbath. If observing sabbath were easy, every Jew and Christian would keep twenty-four hours of it, no sweat. And we will experience the cost of sabbath: time, perhaps money lost, or energy spent on navigating what it means to be faithful stewards of the gift of time in the twenty-first century. But the cost of *not* keeping sabbath is much higher. The tariff on my go-go-go pace was my physical, mental, and spiritual health.

On this journey, I've re-examined myself, my faith, and the world I live in. I've wrestled with what drives me and the discomfort I feel on Sundays that makes me want to run errands and buy. Sabbath means facing the finiteness of things (and us). The eternal part of us (our spirits) are nurtured by *real* living—which has nothing to do with stuff and everything to do with God and community.

Perhaps my most important sabbath learning was realizing how privileged I am to even have time off—the breathing room many minimum-wage workers, shift workers, and families cannot imagine. Traveling this path has made me more aware of the justice message of sabbath and how we, in community, have the power to resist oppressing others together.

Sabbath has given me back a taste of my *real life*. For those with means to cease from work, the myth of being "too busy" to stop for one day, one afternoon, one morning, one hour, or one minute is a defense mechanism that shields us from the hard work of meaning-making. It's much easier to have full calendars and martyr ourselves through the days. It's less work to stay in the American mode of "crazy-busy."

The toughest part of practicing sabbath is letting go of our maladaptive coping so that we may experience fulfillment through an ancient medicine God put in place for everyone. This elixir works—no matter what century, country, or circumstance we find ourselves in.

If we can swing one entire day off (a privilege that others may not have) or one hour off, we ought not turn to the screen. We can use this time to enrich our lives through activities that may not be valued by our culture or economy. We can take a nap, sit in silence alone, pray, read a devotional, attend a church service, enjoy a slow meal with someone, or offer our time to others in a way that doesn't benefit us in a material way. When we don't keep sabbath, we are embezzling time from ourselves, as Rabbi Heschel reminds us. Time is our only nonrenewable resource. Sabbath, then, helps us to number our days rightly.

Observing sabbath is scary. Our broken records tell us that slowing down is lazy or useless or wasteful or leads to death. We've been taught to believe that all the stuff that we make, do, and buy will save us. But God knows better, and we should too.

Sabbath, Reshaped

My fledgling sabbaths are still not where I want them to be, but I remind myself not to keep score. Instead, I have realized how my new sabbaths resemble those of my youth, minus the braces and teenage angst. My intention and awareness have shifted toward noticing God's presence in stillness, devotion, and community. I may not hole up in a dark room for twenty-four hours and meditate on scriptures—I wouldn't even recommend that—but I know that I can't tend to the sacred garden within and around me without stepping out of everyday life.

In addition to a formal Sunday (or any day of the week) practice, I'm a big fan of "sabbath moments," which are sacred glimpses in regular time—like a rainbow on a Thursday afternoon or a conversation with a close friend. Sabbath moments are a good place to start. Once I felt ready to stretch those moments into an hour, an afternoon, or a day, I compiled the following list of ten helpful sabbath practices. The next chapter and appendix contain more details about how to get started, including practical suggestions.

1. Step away from the phone. (Thanks, Rabbi Bach.)
2. Practice humility. I am not the Creator; the world will not fall apart without me.

3. Revisit sabbath scriptures for their essence, not their legalism.

4. Avoid unhelpful self-talk. There's no need for the "lazy" labels when I'm doing something that doesn't move the needle materially.

5. Be intentional about rest. Taking a nap is sabbath. Quiet time and solitude help me listen to God.

6. Attend worship with a devotional intention. Envision it as a necessary fuel-up. No more to-do lists during sermons. I can allow myself to praise God with all my being, offering gratitude and utter devotion, bringing forth my confessions and intercessions sincerely.

7. Relish time in community (I only have this moment!). Be present and give thanks for my gathered tribes of family, friends, church, neighbors, and strangers.

8. Think twice about shopping or dining out on the sabbath. *Everyone* deserves time off. My wallet is a powerful tool in resisting the oppression of others.

9. Share my fledgling (or expert) sabbath practice with others, just as Judaism has been so generous in sharing its tried-and-true spiritual technology. Sabbath was created for all.

10. Remember the meaning of *wabi-sabi*, and seek presence over perfection. Sabbath is *flexible*. Find the balance between firm and fluid boundaries.

Above all, let's lean into wonder, awe, and *menuchah*. Our lives depend on it, for sabbath's sake.

9

CRAFTING YOUR OWN
SABBATH PLAN

Time is the country in which all spiritual practices live and breathe.
—WAYNE MULLER, *THE SABBATH*

Wonder is not reserved for the young.
—WILL BOWEN, *TO YOU, LOVE GOD*

National Public Radio has a weekly news quiz show called, "Wait Wait . . . Don't Tell Me!" hosted by the quick-witted Peter Sagal. Each episode features a segment called "Not My Job." For this portion of the hour, celebrity guests—ranging from scholars to rappers to stunt drivers—answer questions that have *nothing* to do with their day jobs. Absurdity ensues.

Listening to famous people wing it on topics they know nothing about is normalizing; it signifies our common humanity. We feel anxious when we don't know the answer—and we don't want to seem incompetent—but we can't know everything about everything.

This same attitude must be applied to the mysticism of sabbath-keeping. We are not the creators and maintainers of this world; we aren't privy to all the mechanics that went into "Let there be light." God said it, and it happened. We don't need to know how it works, just that God intended it. It's OK to shrug our shoulders politely with an "I don't know" humility. God knows. We only need to offer witness and pay attention.

The Busy Myth

We think if we work hard enough, we'll accomplish everything that needs to get done. Not true. When we die, our inboxes will still be full, the junk drawer will still be messy, and laundry will pile up. We cannot afford to wait for everything to be finished before we do the real "work" of life. Instead, we should rejoice in the fact that it's all a beautiful mess anyway.

Our days can't be numbered rightly with to-do lists. Instead, we should yield to fulfillment through quiet time, worship, spiritual practice, and spending time with the people we love.

We shouldn't "busy" ourselves through a life we *think* we're living.

A Blank Sabbath Canvas

Picture forty Christians, ages three to eighty, in a mountainside conference room. They are sitting at six-foot plastic tables with giant pieces of blank foam board before them. Some are related by blood or adoption; others are friends or partners or spouses. A few came by themselves. They've been brought together for a rare intergenerational gathering on sabbath design.

After a morning plenary on the basics of sabbath (rest, worship, and community), its scripture, history, meaning, and obstacles, Fred and I asked the group to draw, color, paste, or write what their ideal sabbath might look like outside the intentional retreat space we'd enjoyed that weekend. Stacks of magazines, boxes of markers, crayons, colored pencils, scissors, and glue awaited them. They could write words and phrases, draw, or cut out pictures from magazines to offer a visual representation of how they wanted their day to look. They had one hour to craft their sabbath.

Chaos broke out among the adults. Hands were raised, and Fred and I went over to table after table to appease parents who *insisted* that their nuclear families would never agree on what sabbath would look like for them as a unit. Other grown-ups were at a loss: where would they start? The retired adults struggled with how to delineate sabbath time from what now felt like endless days stretched before them.

But the kids got it *immediately.*

While the adults panicked, the children feverishly colored, drew, cut, pasted, and dreamed *the entire hour.* Their brains and hearts and hands didn't stop—and they relished the idea that they could use their imagination to explore and explain how they'd spend sacred time. What they wished for was telling. Each child offered the *same* response to sabbath: Their art depicted more *quality* time with their parents, siblings, friends, and God.

The kids nailed it. They drew pictures of their families together, playing outside; competing in board games, or just doing nothing. They cut out animals, flowers, and happy words and talked about how all of it was God's. They mentioned that they loved church because their friends were there and it was a place that made them feel accepted and loved. The kids relished the opportunity to imagine the possibilities of sabbath, while the adults defaulted to terror. They couldn't get over the physical, emotional, cultural, and economic obstacles to shaping the sabbath day.

That day, the children taught the lesson, leading the adults and offering us a take-home reminder of what we had learned. They inspired us to view sabbath through a child's eyes: playing with no goal in sight; meeting God in nature, animals, and people we love; frittering away time in such a way that is counterintuitive but life-giving.

Our Permission Slip

Sometimes, we need permission to start doing something, to keep doing something, or to stop doing something. We have been granted sabbath as a gift from God, who has ordained it and made it so. Our formal permission slip to keep sabbath is found in Genesis 2:2-3 and Exodus 20:8-11.

Print these verses out, write *PERMISSION SLIP FROM GOD* with a permanent marker at the top of the sheet, and put it on the refrigerator.

Get SMART

Experts disagree on the actual percentages, but most concur that the odds of achieving a goal increase when it is written down. Though sabbath shouldn't necessarily be added to a list of life goals in the material sense of success—like landing the perfect job or owning a vacation home—sabbath can benefit from the SMART goal-writing method.[1] SMART stands for **S**pecific, **M**easurable, **A**chievable, **R**elevant, and **T**ime-bound. Envisioning a sabbath plan (whether with crayons, foam board, or a word processor) helps keep it in the forefront of your mind. If the SMART method speaks to you, use one or all of its criteria to begin defining the parameters of your sabbath practice. If the creative vision board activity is more your thing, go in that direction. Remember that the *intention* (and follow-up) of these practices is what matters.

The trick to any goal-planning is to set yourself up to win. Should this be your first go of sabbath, don't write that you want to observe a strict twenty-four hours in a mountain cave while doing a headstand atop hot coals. There's no need to transform yourself into a wilderness ascetic on day one. Ease into it. If you overdo it, you're more likely to drop the practice all together. Remember: You get to start afresh each week. Try something different each sabbath.

Let your loved ones know about your sabbath practice so that they can support (and join!) you. You are not selfish because you want to take a weekly sabbath, especially if you are a parent or a caregiver for a loved one. Remember that modeling sabbath gives others permission to do so too. I've found that children love the idea of sabbath because they long for unstructured time for wonder, play, and quiet. They, especially, need you to show them (and they can show you) that it can—and should—be done.

The following is an example of a SMART sabbath goal. You can adapt it for your purposes—this is merely to show you how one goal might look.

Specific. I want to observe one hour of sabbath rest. For me, this means quiet time in solitude with God each Sunday evening at my home. During that hour, I will find a comfortable chair, limit the noise around me, and put my cell phone on silent and out of sight and reach. If I have an entire room I can use, I will post a sticky note on the door that I am practicing sabbath rest and am not to be bothered, unless someone is on fire. I will use the hour of rest to be still (15 minutes), read scripture (15 minutes), pray (15 minutes), and practice deep breathing (15 minutes). As the Spirit moves, I can practice one or all of these ways of resting during the hour. If I feel restless, I can also choose to write, draw, knit, or read a book during this time. These are merely guidelines for spending one hour resting by myself in silence with God.

Measurable. I will measure my progress each week by briefly journaling about what happened during the hour and how I felt. I will continue to journal throughout the week (even if it's just one sentence or a phrase) to determine how this restful time with God is impacting my life.

Achievable. To accomplish this sabbath goal, I will block out the time on my family calendar, my work calendar, and/or my digital calendar. I'm going to inform my family, friends, and children about this hour of rest, solitude, and silence. I will encourage them to practice it too, if they'd like, and I will help them hold the space.

Relevant. I've been feeling stressed at my job and bringing a lot of work home. I'm inundated with projects, along with caring for my children, parents, spouse, and home. This is a goal that is relevant for me right now. I feel disconnected from God, spiritually dry and drained. This hour is a good start to reconnecting with myself and God.

Time-bound. I will accomplish this goal in the next month, with one hour each week for four hours total. At the end of the month, I will assess whether it was helpful by checking in with myself and reading my journal entries. If I find the practice useful, this might be a first step in my progress toward establishing a regular quiet-time routine on Sundays. Once the month concludes, I can also make any changes and adaptations necessary and set another SMART goal for the subsequent month.

Chunking Versus Twenty-Four Hours

In writing this book, I discovered the greatest sabbatarian debate: what day, how much time, and what do you do? Must you observe sabbath on a Sunday or Saturday? Does it have to be twenty-four hours? Is it just worship—or can it be outside time, rest, play, shared meals, or activism? If someone works weekends, can he or she take another whole day for sabbath, or spread it out in chunks throughout the week? After all my reading, the answer to all these questions is yes.

Most religious and spiritual scholars and congregational leaders agree that starting a sabbath practice *whenever* we can, *wherever* we can, *however* we can, and with *whatever* we can is good. If you can swing a twenty-four-hour mixture of sabbath rest, worship, and community on a Sunday—try it. If you need to wade in slowly, spreading bits of sabbath throughout the week—do it. The point is that you start somewhere, and perhaps you will love it so much that you can't imagine what you ever did without it.

As with any new habit or path, we must set ourselves up for success. Tiny bites, one Sunday at a time. As the house-cleaning, meal-making, chaos-diffusing self-help guru The FlyLady says, "You are never behind. Jump in where you are."

Prioritizing

Whether you are a full-day or a chunking sabbatarian, you must learn to re-prioritize and set boundaries. Think about what you can take care of prior to sabbath to help free your mind for rest, quiet time, devotional practices, and time in community. What will help you stay mindful and present?

If something comes up during your designated sabbath time, ask yourself, *Can this wait?* Remind yourself that not everything is an emergency. Help yourself (and your family) prioritize "urgent" tasks.

We're in This Together

Accountability can help you stay focused and not feel so alone. Practicing together also offers space for sharing, collaborating, and reflecting on what's working well and where you still need to grow and learn.

Ask your ministry staff about their sabbath practices. Perhaps your interest will prompt them to lead a small group, scripture study, or sermon series centered on sabbath. See if you can organize for your church's sanctuary to remain open and quiet for silent prayer time on Sunday before or just after worship. Offer to be someone's "sabbath buddy," the accountability system used by Kate Rademacher. Check in with your sabbath buddy via phone, email, or in-person before and after the sabbath. Don't underestimate what a little note of encouragement (both giving and receiving) can manifest.

Think about how you may be of service in helping others keep sabbath. Respect the sabbath boundaries of your pastor and others. Volunteer to gather quotes, scripture, or sabbath suggestions to share on the worship bulletin, in the newsletter, on the church's social media accounts, or on a bulletin board in the educational rooms of your parish.

Ego Is the Enemy

Unless you are an on-duty surgeon, nurse, firefighter, paramedic, or police officer; the President of the United States; or a scientist within twenty-four hours of finding the cure for cancer, your work *really* can wait. Working 24/7, answering that midnight email, or taking that phone call during a family meal is not going to make the difference between life and death. Sabbath calls you to practice humility and imbibe some wisdom from a cheesy Carrie Underwood song: Let Jesus "take the wheel" for a while.

Fighting your own ego may be difficult because your devices, with their endless pinging and buzzing, make you feel as though you are indispensable. They are designed to create the urgency that *someone* or *something* needs your attention *at all times*. This urgency can lead to information overload, exhaustion, busyness, franticness, chaos, stress, no quality time with loved ones, and a stale spiritual life.

Sabbath is God's antidote for what ails you spiritually. It's the one day (or one moment) per week when you can and need to remove yourself from the demands of the world. Then, you have the space to ponder the big stuff (in a good way); to play; to wonder; and to delight in God, in nature, and in others. Remember that God—the One who has unlimited time, resources, and energy—*still* took a day for rest.

Change the Record

You can flip the must-go, must-do records in your head with a SMART goal or simply follow the steps below, which are a bit more fluid. If you get stuck, begin again with step one. Each day, hour, and moment is a new opportunity for sabbath.

If you want sabbath to feel less scientific and measurable, use these prompts to explore through writing, thinking, discussion, or prayer. Check in often. Using an adapted form of Ignatian spirituality to see where you felt God's presence, what brings you energy, and what drains you. You can also use these three prompts a chaplain once taught me: I feel hopeful about . . . . I feel anxious about. . . . I feel curious about. . . .

1. What's going on in your life that makes you crave sabbath? What event, circumstance, or person drew you to reading this book and learning more about creating a sabbath practice for yourself?

2. Set a sabbath intention for yourself or your family. Find a quiet space, and bring a notebook or a blank piece of paper or poster board and something to write or draw with. Together or separately, dream of what you want sabbath to bring to your life. Is it more quiet or contemplative time? Prayer time? Scripture study? Sleep? Worship? Reconnecting with God, yourself, or family? More time outdoors? Time to read or engage in creativity?

3. Once you've decided on an intention (or intentions), write it out clearly. My sabbath intention is to. . . .

4. Now, how might you keep this sabbath intention? What's the method? For example, if your intention is rest, determine how, specifically, you might get it. If it's worship, brainstorm ways you might engage in devotional practices with God. Is your intention community? Be specific about the ways in which you can keep and fulfill your intention.

5. Make a plan and guard it. How will you hold yourself accountable? Who do you need to inform about your plan so that he or she can help you stay accountable? For the next week, I am going to (name the intention and the method) on the sabbath.

6. How did it go? Write down how you felt—what worked and what didn't. Where did you feel God's presence? What do you need to tweak, if anything?

7. Now that you've thought more about and/or reshaped the plan, commit to two weeks of sabbath practice. For the next two weeks, I am going to (name the intention and the method) on the sabbath.

8. Again, examine. What energized you about steps 2–7? What challenged you? What makes you hopeful/anxious/curious about sabbath?

9. Go back to your pre-work (step one) and why you began searching for sabbath in the first place. How do you feel now? Notice how you've changed. Do you need help keeping the same intention and method? How have you grown in your sabbath practice? If you feel you haven't grown in noticing or keeping some form of sabbath, return to step one. Remember, nothing is written in stone. You can tweak your intention and method anytime; you and your needs are not static.

10. *Wabi-sabi.* Perfection is not an option. Keep tweaking, adjusting, and checking in.

Remember to enjoy the process. I am a goal gal; I don't much like the process, but I know that it shapes me more than the result. Allow yourself to wonder in the exploration of an ancient gift given to you from God. This is *your journey;* take delight in it.

APPENDIX: RESOURCES FOR YOUR SABBATH JOURNEY

The dream of my life
Is to lie down by a slow river
—MARY OLIVER, "ENTERING THE KINGDOM"

Scripture Readings on Sabbath

Use these in your own personal journey of sabbath. Explore the ancient readings and what they mean for you today.

- Genesis 2:2-3
- Exodus 20:8-11
- Exodus 31:12-17
- Deuteronomy 5:15
- Isaiah 58:13-14
- Ezekiel 20:12, 20
- Matthew 11:28
- Mark 2:23-27

Shabbat Blessing

Blessed are you, Adonai our God, Sovereign of the universe, who hallows us with mitzvot, commanding us to kindle the light of Shabbat. (Visit www. reformjudaism.org for more information.)

Sabbath Prayer

Creator God, you have given me the weekly gift of sabbath. Help me to step out of this chaotic world and into sacred space and time. May I keep my intention of rest, worship, and community—seeking always to listen for your voice and to number my days rightly. Amen.

Ideas for Rest, Worship, and Community

Rest

- Put your phone away. Silence it, place it in a drawer, or ask someone to keep it for you. Use your phone's emergency call settings so that only your children, spouse, or family members can reach you *if they have to.*
- Take a nap.
- Lie down in your yard, on your porch, or in a public park. Watch the clouds. Then, close your eyes and listen. Offer a prayer of gratitude.
- Make list of things for which you are grateful.
- Write God a letter.
- Sit in your favorite chair, and ask God to join you in that space. Do a puzzle, Sudoku, crossword, or color in a coloring book. (I suggest *Praying with Mandalas: A Colorful, Contemplative Practice* by Sharon Seyfarth Garner.) Remember that God is with you.
- Take a mindful walk; notice the textures and sounds around you.
- Take a sick day.
- Read in bed. Allow yourself to doze off.
- Go to an afternoon matinee by yourself.
- Visit DoNothingFor2Minutes.com.
- Keep a sabbath jar. Write down your sabbath ideas and activities on slips of paper. Fold and place them in the jar to retrieve when you need to jump-start your practice.
- Set a timer for five minutes, and practice deep breathing for that amount of time.

- Sit in a room by yourself for fifteen minutes—no phone, no books. Be silent. Pray. When you become restless, use the alphabet to name the people, circumstances, and blessings for which you're thankful (think big *and* small).
- Do something creative: weave, knit, paint, write, scrapbook, draw, make music, or color.
- Practice some form of movement: dance, stretching, or yoga. (I suggest *Holy Listening with Breath, Body, and the Spirit* by Whitney R. Simpson.)
- Try fasting from information: no social media, Internet, TV, radio, or newspaper for one morning, one hour, one afternoon, or one day.
- Invest in a meditation sandbox, mini waterfall, or prayer beads. (I suggest *A Bead and a Prayer: A Beginner's Guide to Protestant Prayer Beads* by Kristen E. Vincent.) Use these tangible instruments to center yourself in God's presence.
- Be silent in nature. Listen for God.
- Take a long bath.
- Spend an entire day in your pajamas.
- Sit by, gaze at, swim in, or play in water (a baby pool, in-ground pool, creek, pond, lake, river, ocean, inlet, bay, or waterway).
- Do laundry mindfully. Give God thanks for each article of clothing, for water, for electricity, and for modern machinery.
- Take a drive in the country with the windows down and the radio up. Sing your heart out!
- Walk a path, trail, or labyrinth. Let the Spirit speak to you in ways that don't require words.

Worship

- Attend a worship service—one you are familiar with (your home church, if you have one) or one you've never been to (a church nearby, a new denomination, etc.).
- Focus on your devotional intention toward God during a worship service; offer yourself grace if/when your mind wanders.

- During a worship service, give God thanks, praise, and adoration. Confess the spaces where you need spiritual mending and ask God to intercede—especially in matters beyond your control. Pray that you will be refueled and infused with the Spirit for the week ahead.
- Volunteer with your community's children's worship programs (for example, children's church or Sunday school). See worship through the eyes of a child.
- Sing your favorite hymns at church or at home.
- Listen to devotional music in the car during your commute.
- Attend a Taizé or contemplative worship and prayer service.
- Learn to play (or revisit) an instrument; offer your music in praise to God.
- Worship outside.
- Observe the church's liturgical rhythm (Advent, Christmas, Epiphany, Lent, Holy Week, Easter, Pentecost, and Ordinary Time).
- Try a different form of prayer (contemplative, centering, *lectio divina*, meditative, extemporaneous, or using prayer book).
- Make a space at home where you can offer prayers of thanksgiving, confession, and intercession to God.

Community

- Share a meal with someone you know well.
- Share a meal with someone you don't know well.
- Share a meal with a stranger.
- Introduce yourself to one person every day. Repeat his or her name when you learn it and smile.
- Pray for everyone you encounter—those standing in line next to you, workers at a cash register, drivers in traffic. Everyone you see needs prayer.
- Plan a family night, and keep it simple. Bake a frozen pizza and play a game. Talk; laugh; have fun.

- Meet someone at a local park. Take a walk together and catch up without your phones.
- Be intentional about playing with your own children or someone else's. Give little ones your full, undivided attention.
- Start a container garden with your family or neighbors. Grow something easy like herbs. Give God thanks for the bounty of the fruit it yields, and share your harvest abundantly.
- Pay attention to community opportunities listed in your local newspaper. How can you use your time to make your community better for all who live there?
- Be mindful of privilege. If you do not have to work weekends, try to limit your shopping and eating out on the sabbath. Consider the power of your wallet. How might you help others have a day off too?
- Donate what you might have spent on the sabbath for meals or shopping to your church's discretionary fund or a charity of your choice.
- Establish a monthly small-group gathering centered on a theme: prayer, games, art, food, music, books, or nature.
- Meet a friend (or take a group of children, friends, or family) at a local museum. Marvel at the creative gifts God has given us.
- Try an outdoor activity with a small group: biking, hiking, kayaking, canoeing, or swimming.
- Prepare a meal for someone. Don't rush. Pray over and savor each step—and, later, each bite.
- Give a loved one (child or adult) a manicure or pedicure. Remember that Jesus washed his disciples' feet with love and a servant heart.

NOTES

Chapter Two: Sabbath Roots

1. For more information on The Four Questions (*Mah Nishtanah*), visit http://www.reformjudaism.org/jewish-holidays/passover/four-questions.
2. Gloria Eaker, in discussion with the author, May 2016.
3. For more information on the Seventh-Day Adventist Church's sabbath observance, visit https://www.adventist.org/en/information/official-statements/documents/article/go/-/sabbath-observance/.
4. Walter Brueggemann, *Sabbath as Resistance: Saying No to the Culture of Now* (Louisville, KY: Westminster John Knox Press, 2014), 20.
5. Judith Harrow, in discussion with the author, August 2016.
6. Judith Shulevitz, *The Sabbath World: Glimpses of a Different Order of Time* (New York: Random House, 2011), 68.
7. Ana Levy-Lyons, "Sabbath Practice as Political Resistance: Building the Religious Counterculture," *Tikkun*, 27, no. 4 (Fall 2012): 17.
8. Abraham Joshua Heschel, *The Sabbath: Its Meaning for Modern Man* (New York: Farrar, Strauss, and Giroux, 1951), 15.
9. Levy-Lyons, "Sabbath Practice as Political Resistance," 17.
10. Benjamin J. Dueholm, "The war against rest," *The Christian Century*, November 26, 2014, 24.
11. Levy-Lyons, "Sabbath Practice as Political Resistance," 17.
12. Rabbi Larry Bach, in discussion with the author, May 2016.
13. Norman Wirzba, *Living the Sabbath: Discovering Rhythms of Rest and Delight* (Grand Rapids, MI: Brazoz Press, 2006), 33.
14. Heschel, *Sabbath*, 10.
15. Shulevitz, *The Sabbath World*, xxvii.
16. Ibid., 43–44.
17. Ibid., xxv.
18. Ibid., 92.
19. Ibid., 91.
20. Ibid., 94.
21. Matthew Sleeth, MD, *24-6: A Prescription for a Healthier, Happier Life* (Carol Stream, IL: Tyndale House Publishers, 2012), 52.

22. Wayne Muller, *Sabbath: Finding Rest, Renewal, and Delight in Our Busy Lives* (New York: Bantam Books, 1999), 24–25.

23. Richard Lowery, "Sabbath, a 'Little Jubilee,'" *Sabbath*, Christian Reflection: A Series in Faith and Ethics (Baylor, TX: Baylor University Press, 2002), 9–10.

24. David Capes, "The Eighth Day," *Sabbath*, Christian Reflection: A Series in Faith and Ethics (Baylor, TX: Baylor University Press, 2002), 21.

25. Shulevitz, *The Sabbath World*, 93.

26. Muller, *Sabbath*, 77.

27. Shulevitz, *The Sabbath World*, 107.

28. Capes, "The Eighth Day," 20.

29. Shulevitz, *The Sabbath World*, 113.

30. Shulevitz, *The Sabbath World*, 114.

31. Ibid., 121.

32. Ibid., 147.

33. Ibid., 147.

34. Shulevitz, *The Sabbath World*, 143.

35. Ibid., 147.

36. Ibid., 192–3.

37. Donna Schaper, *Sabbath Keeping* (Boston: Cowley Publications, 1999), 47.

Chapter Three: Sabbath, Culture, and the Economy of Frenzy

1. Adam Sternbergh, "Is *Friends* Still the Most Popular Show on TV?" *New York Magazine*, March 21, 2016, http://www.vulture.com/2016/03/20-some things-streaming-friends-c-v-r.html?mid=twitter_nymag.

2. Ibid.

3. Paul Miller, "I'm still here: back online after a year without the internet," *The* Verge, May 1, 2013. http://www.theverge.com/2013/5/1/4279674 /im-still-here-back-online-after-a-year-without-the-internet.

4. Brueggemann, *Sabbath as Resistance*, 10.

5. Karl G. D. Bailey and Arian C. B. Timoti, "Delight or Distraction: An Exploratory Analysis of Sabbath-Keeping Internalization," *Journal of Psychology & Theology* 43, no. 3 (2015): 201.

6. Marla Campbell, "Transformational Rest for Educators," *Christian Education Journal* 9, no. 1 (Spring 2012): 199.

7. Mark Buchanan, "Schedule, Interrupted: Discovering God's time-management technique," *Christianity Today,* February 2006, 44.

8. Ibid., 44.

9. Ibid., 44.

10. Ibid., 44-45.

11. Sleeth, 24-6, 9.

12. Ibid., 35–36.

13. Ibid., 6–7.
14. Shulevitz, *The Sabbath World*, 18–19.
15. Rebecca Lee, "Why it's important to 'refuel' with vacation days," *CBS News*, July 6, 2016. http://www.cbsnews.com/news/tony-schwartz-ceo-the-energy-project-importance-of-vacation-days/.
16. Dan Buettner, *The Blue Zones: 9 Lessons for Living Longer,* Washington: National Geographic Society, 2008.
17. Levy-Lyons, "Sabbath Practice as Political Resistance," 17.
18. Barbara Brown Taylor, "Sabbath Resistance," *The Christian Century,* May 31, 2005, 35.
19. Wirzba, *Living the Sabbath*, 20.
20. Muller, *Sabbath*, 6.
21. Wirzba, 30.
22. Levy-Lyons, "Sabbath Practice as Political Resistance," 18.
23. Ibid., 66.
24. Monica Reed, MD, "Beyond Sleep: Resting the Rest of You," *Vibrant Life* 24, no. 6 (Nov/Dec 2008): 18.

Chapter Four: A Different Calling

1. Kate Rademacher, in discussion with the author, May 2016.
2. To learn more about Kate Rademacher's conversion journey, see *Following the Red Bird: First Steps into a Life of Faith* (Durham, NC: Light Messages Publishing, 2017).
3. For more information on this study, visit http://www.pewforum.org/2015/05/12/americas-changing-religious-landscape/.

Chapter Five: Sabbath as Rest

1. American Time Use Survey News Release, U.S. Bureau of Labor Statistics, https://www.bls.gov/news.release/atus.htm.
2. Monica Reed, "Beyond Sleep," 16.
3. Farris Samarrai, "Doing Something Is Better than Doing Nothing for Most People, Study Shows," *UVA Today,* July 3, 2014, https://news.virginia.edu/content/doing-something-better-doing-nothing-most-people-study-shows.

Chapter Six: Sabbath as Worship

1. Emma Green, "It's Hard to Go to Church," *The* Atlantic, August 23, 2016, http://www.theatlantic.com/politics/archive/2016/08/religious-participation-survey/496940/.
2. Jeff Strickler, "A Minneapolis congregation finds new life through the ancient practice of keeping Sabbath," *Faith & Leadership*, March 22, 2016,

https://www.faithandleadership.com/minneapolis-congregation-finds-new-life-through-ancient-practice-keeping-sabbath.

3. Stanley Hauerwas, "Speaking Christian: A Commencement Address for Eastern Mennonite Seminary," *Mennonite Quarterly Review* 84 (July 2010), https://www.goshen.edu/wp-content/uploads/sites/75/2016/06/July10 Hauerwas.pdf, 1.

Chapter Seven: Sabbath as Community

1. Barbara Brown Taylor, "Sabbath Resistance," *The Christian Century,* May 31, 2005, 35.
2. Ibid.
3. Ibid.
4. Arthur Waskow, "Free Time for a Free People," *The Nation,* December 14, 2000, https://www.thenation.com/article/free-time-free-people/. See also https://theshalomcenter.org/node/1594.
5. Ibid.
6. Dorothy C. Bass, "Christian Formation in and for Sabbath Rest," *Interpretation* 59, no. 1 (January 2005): 37.
7. Ibid., 26.
8. David Keller, "Reading Living Water: The Integral Place on Contemplative Prayer in Christian Formation," *Sewanee Theological Review* 50, no. 3 (Pentecost 2007): 411.
9. David Pacchioli, "Bonhoeffer's Dilemma," *Penn State News,* May 1, 2005, http://news.psu.edu/story/140578/2000/05/01/research/bonhoeffer%E2%80%99s-dilemma.
10. Ibid.

Chapter Nine: Crafting Your Sabbath Plan

1. George T. Doran, "There's a S.M.A.R.T. way to write management's goals and objectives," Management Review 70, no. 11 (November 1981): 35–36.

For those who hunger for deep spiritual experience . . .

The Academy for Spiritual Formation® is an experience of disciplined Christian community emphasizing holistic spirituality—nurturing body, mind, and spirit. The program, a ministry of The Upper Room®, is ecumenical in nature and meant for all those who hunger for a deeper relationship with God, including both lay and clergy persons. Each Academy fosters spiritual rhythms—of study and prayer, silence and liturgy, solitude and relationship, rest and exercise. With offerings of both Two-Year and Five-Day models, Academy participants rediscover Christianity's rich spiritual heritage through worship, learning, and fellowship. The Academy's commitment to an authentic spirituality promotes balance, inner and outer peace, holy living and justice living—God's shalom.

Faculty trained in the wide breadth of Christian spirituality and practice provide content and guidance at each session of The Academy. Academy faculty presenters come from seminaries, monasteries, spiritual direction ministries, and pastoral ministries or other settings and are from a variety of traditions.

The Academy Recommends program seeks to highlight content that aligns with the Academy's mission to provide resources and settings where pilgrims encounter the teachings, sustaining practices, and rhythms that foster attentiveness to God's Spirit and therefore help spiritual leaders embody Christ's presence in the world.

The ACADEMY RECOMMENDS program seeks to highlight content that aligns with the Academy's mission to provide resources and settings where pilgrims encounter the teachings, sustaining practices, and rhythms that foster attentiveness to God's Spirit and therefore help spiritual leaders embody Christ's presence in the world.

academy.upperroom.org